SCOPES
OF
DIMENSIONS

HOW TO EXPERIENCE
MULTI-DIMENSIONAL REALITY

VYWAMUS

Channeled by Janet McClure

Edited by Lillian Harben

SCOPES OF DIMENSIONS
How to Experience
Multi-Dimensional Reality

Vywamus, Channeled by Janet McClure

Copyright ©1989 by the Tibetan Foundation

Published and printed by

800-450-0985
www.lighttechnology.com

PO Box 3540
Flagstaff, AZ 86003
publishing@lighttechnology.net

About the Author

Janet McClure, an exceptional channel, devotes her full time and energies to the conscious channeling of spiritual beings. She shares their teachings of truth and understanding to aid in humanity's transformation.

Janet had been studying intensively for many years with a spiritual teacher and had received her Doctor of Metaphysics from The Brotherhood of the White

Temple. She had already dedicated her life to the service of the Cosmic Plan when she was asked by Djwhal Khul to assist him in aiding humanity by being a conscious channel for his energies and spiritual teachings. Djwhal was responding to a request from Sanat Kumara, the Planetary Logos who ensouls the earth, to return to his earth contacts and once again aid humanity as he had done forty years earlier through Alice Bailey and her books.

Djwhal knew that channeling would flow easily for Janet as she had extensive channeling experience in previous lives and had been a channeling teacher in Ancient Egypt. Janet enthusiastically put aside her familiar and comfortable world of business and committed herself to this new mission. Being an Aries, Janet's nature is to move forward with her new age awareness, secure in the knowledge of the support she would receive from the Source.

After channeling for two years, Janet was introduced by Djwhal to the cosmic being Vywamus, a caring and loving being who is a light aspect of Sanat Kumara. Vywamus was attracted to the beautiful light of the Earth and now continues the work with Janet that Djwhal began in 1982. Djwhal is now focusing his energies toward the plans for the New Age on Earth.

Vywamus encourages the training of channels as he believes channeling to be the single most important step one can take to move forward in their evolution. Concerning her own evolution, Janet says, "The benefits I have received by channeling in terms of clearing blocked areas for myself are enormous. My evolution has accelerated greatly through the channeling process." Janet is joyful for the 180 degree change her life has taken since she first began to channel for Djwhal Khul.

INTRODUCTION TO VYWAMUS

My Friends,

I, Djwhal Khul, have the privilege of introducing to you Vywamus - a great Being who has come among us to serve during these critical, yet marvelous, times when humanity seeks to evolve into spiritual consciousness, casting off the outworn "forms" and moving in greater light into the New Age. Many spiritual teachers are appearing to help mankind and Mother Earth make this transition as painless and clear as possible and at as high a level as possible.

Vywamus, then, is One of a very elevated consciousness. Vywamus is an evolved aspect of Sanat Kumara (our Planetary Logos) who ensouls the earth and all upon it and within it. The Earth, in effect, is being "held together" by his focus of consciousness.. At a still higher level of this consciousness is Vywamus. He can be equated to the "higher self," as we sometimes refer to it, or the soul of Sanat Kumara.

Vywamus evolved to his present "position" through the physical chain - just as humanity has chosen to do. Vywamus chose to express in physical existence aeons ago, and did this on a planet similar to Earth. While in physical existence he was offered the opportunity to be a channel for higher energies, and thus serving gained clear perceptions and quickly passed on to the spiritual plane. This was accomplished after only thirty-seven incarnations on the physical.

Now, in his great love, he has chosen to assist mankind. An exceptional channel, Janet McClure, brings through this explanation of the dimensions, which Vywamus offers to mankind with his love.

DJWHAL KHUL

CHAPTERS

INTRODUCTION

There is a gate or a door that has been opened which is allowing a dimensional stretch that will access for the Earth a clearer, a more encompassing, and for most on the Earth, a happier way of existence. This is the beginning of a comprehensive discussion on dimensions, a means to understand dimensions, to explore them, to give a series of exercises in regard to them and a bridging of them. In short, we begin now a dimensional journey that will allow you to access structure < which is the flow of the dimensions in a manner that you've never thought possible. It is truly an exciting new beginning for the Earth and for you that are reading this.

I am Vywamus, a spiritual teacher, and I invite you now on a journey, to come with me to venture forth in your understanding and to learn more about life by doing so. I know that you've had many questions about why is the Earth the way it is? Why is humanity seemingly at a point where conditions on the Earth cause frustration, concern that soon there may not be an Earth? Why does it seem to be this way? What can each one do to bring about the peace and the type of Earth experience that is desired.

Although this journey is to be a comprehensive one, it is but a glimpse of what can be understood through a complete study of the dimensions. I hope that it will awaken within you a desire to know more, a response that says, "yes, I am ready to make the effort now to bring together within me a uniting of all of my skills, talents and abilities to bring about the type of Earth that is desirable. I say to you my friends, this is the dawning of your New Age, let us explore it through what I am calling the dimensions. Or through the structural flow of the Source itself as it unites with possibilities, alternatives and then utilizes these possibilities within physical existence itself.

There is nothing mysterious about creation, it is laid out clearly in front of us, you simply need the eyes to see and the way that one sees is definitely through the heart area, your heart must be open to the vision of peace, to the vision of understanding, to the vision of cooperation, to the vision of allowing the manifestation of a peaceful new Earth. Let us explore it together in great detail, seeking to see how each day can bring you the opportunity to realize the new Earth potential.

Thank you,

Vywamus

CHAPTER 1

DIMENSIONS DEFINED

Dimensions are a means to organize existence, to bring about divine order. They hold consciousness in a way that allows it to be able to function clearly, easily and with a minimum of resistance. Let me give you the following example of a dimensions in order that you may understand it more clearly.

Let us say then that you have recently moved into a house as a newlywed. Now the house is not very large, let us say it has 3 bedrooms and 2 baths and a kitchen, dining area and living room. You furnish it and life is comfortable within it but then you have a child. After the first child you still have enough room but you notice that the child's paraphernalia takes up a great deal of room. There are the diapers, the crib for the child and the clothing, the playpen and toys but that's fine, you have the room.

Let us say you have a second child a couple of years later and in the meantime the first child is two years old and now has a room by himself and has a bed and toys and so forth. Now your 3 bedroom house is very full and time passes and there is a third child born. Now is when the house gets crowded. The middle child must move in with the older child to make room for the baby and that is what is done but it seems to you that its time to look for a new house. This structure, this house that you have is no longer able to hold all of the consciousness that lives there without a sense of crowding. Let us assume that you have sufficient abundance so you go shopping for a house and you find a 4 bedroom house. Not only does it have 4 bedrooms but they are larger, there is now an extra bath and there is a family room that wasn't there before, perhaps a bigger yard for the children. Now your structure is larger and you are again comfortable within your house.

Cnd

Now, this is an important analogy because the Earth has recently had an opportunity to enlarge or go to a larger structure, to move into a larger house, if you will, because it has become so crowded with consciousness that it needed more room. Now a fallacious belief says that your planet cannot hold as many people as there are here, that there isn't physical room for them but that is a 3rd dimensional concept. What is needed is not more physical room on your planet but a larger structure that contains a great deal more of the 4th dimension which has a flowing concept that the 3rd dimension does not have.

4th

In this material that I am introducing now we are going to analyze and talk about dimensions rather completely. We are going to look at them in a lot of detail. We are going to give you examples of how to use dimensions and exercises to help you understand your own placement within the dimensions. We are, in short, going to explore dimensions rather completely. Your Earth has literally turned a corner in its ability to access a larger use of the dimensions. As in our example so many children have been born now into this physical format and the planet is so full of consciousness that it is expanding its structure by being able to access the dimensions in a whole different manner.

Now we are going to make it as clear as possible what the dimensions really represent *Di's* so that you can see that you really function interdimensionally all of the time but what I mean by a whole different way of referencing the dimensions then is how you use these dimensions, the means by which your *conc* consciousness can access dimensions and thus flow within them.

It's the difference between skating a little bit as an ice skater perhaps and being able to enter the Olympics because you can use the skates and the environment within which you skate in a way in which they are compatible.

You see, one must recognize the environment which is the dimensional flow so completely and be so familiar with it and how to use it that you become an expert or someone that is able to be that Olympic star within this clearly defined environment.

Now, perhaps I need to explain that I'm not talking about a type of athletics but I am

5

talking about your clear understanding of what is called the divine plan for the Earth and how that works and how to access the parts and aspects of self to use the opportunities given to you now on the Earth. The goal again is to understand your "house" or the dimensional system so that you can use it in any way that you choose and of course the ultimate way to choose to use it is clearly or with an alignment into the plan as it was conceived for the Earth.

In the fullest sense you are all Olympic stars, you have so much ability, so many potentials. You have not even tapped a fraction of who you are, not yet, thus here on the Earth there is now the opportunity to explore in a manner that is so exciting that I feel very privileged to bring this material to you.

If you study the following material and do the exercises you will be able to understand yourself as never before, to understand others much more completely, to communicate with others more fully, to communicate with yourself as never before and to use you abilities in a way that will access for you or bring to you more and more cosmic opportunities, more and more of a statement of who you are from a very cosmic level.

Self Structure You can see who you are because you have right out in front of you now on the Earth a structure that organizes or puts into alignment all parts of you. When you understand what this means and how to access all parts of self within this structure in a flowing and an aligned manner it will bring to you anything that you choose to put into your life. If someone says to you "how would you like to be a concert violinist?" You will know exactly how you would go about using the concert violinists ability within you (and yes, my friend, you have those abilities within you) because you will understand the structure and how your abilities and potentialities are lined up within that structure. You may choose to say to that person, "I don't believe that being a concert violinist is what my Soul has chosen for this lifetime but I could be one if I believed that choice was in alignment with my Soul's purpose."

In other words, laid out within structure is your own unlimitedness. Now that is not a opposition, a statement that seems to contain an opposition. Clearly in order to see what unlimitedness is, you must organize and understand all of your potential. That doesn't mean that you will see every facet of unlimitedness because the very nature of it means that it cannot ever be all seen but you will see the organizational part of how to use it and you will sense how organization cooperates with itself and allows harmony, allows communication, allows integration, allows a creative response, allows divine choices. Allowingness thus is stimulated through the sense of security that comes in understanding an organized structure or what has been called dimensions.

We will begin our journey by talking briefly about each dimension and giving you an exercise within each dimension for you to access it. This will be the first step in our dimensional journey, we will give you a key phrase or two about each dimension so that you may understand it more fully.

FIRST DIMENSION

The first dimension is a passageway or a corridor which leads to a completion. There never was a time when nothing existed. Our Source has always been but there are points of completion, points of merging and thus points where consciousness unites its aspects and creates a unification of understanding. These points are called the first dimension.

EXERCISE: Seek to remember a time when you completed something. Perhaps you graduated from high school or college. Go back to how you felt then, seek to see what your feelings were at this time of completion. They were probably varied, there was a sense of accomplishment perhaps, there may have been some wondering about what lay beyond this point but through something that you have experienced sense to see this completion and how you felt about it. Many aspects fit together at that time, many areas in which you had learned and grown in your understanding came together.

Also at that point the very nature of this completion or this first dimension activates another corridor which leads then to the second dimension. As you seek in this exercise to feel what you felt at this point of completion you will note that there is for many of you a movement, a flow stimulated from focusing on that completion. The very nature of the first dimension spirals you through a flow movement into the second dimension. In other words, as you perhaps focus on completing high school you begin to stimulate how you felt about going or not going to college or whatever was the next step for you. The first dimension and your emotional responses to it stimulates the connection with the second dimension. We will give you in each dimension a key word for that dimension. The first key word in the first dimension is ***Completion*** .

SECOND DIMENSION

The first dimension is the only new beginning stimulator that exists. There was never a time when nothing existed. There always was something that was stimulating a new level of awareness or a new beginning which is what the second dimension means. Thus our key for the second dimension is ***New Beginning.*** Many times there is still an active state or an integrative state from the first dimension as the second dimension is contacted. In other words, you are still cleaning up your act, your completion of the previous level as the new one is stimulated. For example: in college you may still have to take your final examinations but already there are those that come to interview you at college and you may have the opportunity of going to work for them. A new beginning is already being stimulated by the completion of the previous level of learning.

EXERCISE: As you think about the previous example that you used as a completion now begin to see how that completion stimulated the next step and emotionally flow into it. What lay beyond that completion for you? What was that new level that was stimulated by the former completion? As you allow yourself to remember through the emotional body certain emotions will surface and it is possible for you to remember in a way through the emotions that stimulates a response that is more complete than if you just seek to remember it through your mental focus or mental body.

Your mind, many times, tunes out your emotional responses because they may not have been something that seemed to the mental to be especially appropriate. One example might be someone that goes away to college and is rather homesick for a while but looking back on it mentally many years later many times that will not be remembered. If you look back through your emotional responses though, you will begin to remember that homesickness. Now why is that important? Well, being homesick means that your resolution of the former area or your completion of that first level isn't finished yet, you're still resolving it and it is perhaps important to know that you may have as many as five hundred levels of completion that you are not yet completely through with or you haven't resolved. Now, that's important. Look at it this way - you have a plate on a stick and it represents the completion and when you have completed a level your plate will spin eternally, in balance, and you won't have to keep re-balancing it. Now if you think about having 500 plates out there and every once and a while because you haven't yet balanced them you must give them some attention, then you can see that it's rather wasting your energy. You are limiting your present opportunity if emotionally you have not yet allowed that plate or that level to be completed.

I have stated that for all of you the emotional body is the one that needs to be balanced. It is the one that is the most needful of understanding more clearly. It is the one which in many of you needs to be more mature. Not all of you use your emotional body in the same manner. Some of you focus on the mental body and don't acknowledge your emotions very much. You could say you bury your emotional responses, not feeling they are appropriate, not believing that they are very helpful in your life. There are others of you who focus on the emotions to such an extent that you often wipe out at inappropriate times the effectiveness of the mental body, you actually turn off your head. Your emotions can do that rather easily, they do it at times when

11

you get caught up in an emotion - when it literally pulls you back into one of those 500 focuses that you are trying to complete.

Now, those focuses are not just all out there one at a time, many times you have to go through one to get to another so it uses all of your energy and your emotional reserve to literally "fight" your way emotionally from one level to another. There is a struggle to straighten out each plate and then go deeper and deeper until your energy and your emotional reserves are absolutely drained and absolutely gone.

Well, what to do about it? There is a way to straighten all of this out. We will talk about it when we have completed our understanding of the dimensions, when we have awakened your conceptual grasp of what dimensions are in a clear enough manner that you can use that conceptual understanding to balance the emotions as you seek to resolve all of the levels of what I call plates that are still spinning and still not yet resolved.

Dimensions one and two are used in conjunction with the other dimensions but not in exactly the same way. We could say they are the corridors, the doors and the windows of the other dimensions and they are necessary. We could also say they are the connection between all of the other dimensions.

Now, I have divided our dimensional journey into 9 pieces and it is rather like cutting a pie into 9 slices, if we wanted to we could cut it into 12 or we could cut it into 6 or we could cut it into 24 but for the purpose of this material I am cutting it into 9 pieces.

In your physical life the dimensions that affect you the most are the 3rd through the 6th and of course the 1st and the 2nd as a part of those other dimensions.

Let us continue now with our dimensional discussion, moving into dimension three.

Dimension 3 - key word ***Magnification***. When you came to the Earth you discovered a planet that has sat very securely and deeply within the 3rd dimension. Now that is changing, the planet is lightening and is moving and beginning to enter the 4th dimension but in sequential time in the past it has been quite a "heavy" planet as far as a dimensional focus was concerned. It is necessary to understand the 3rd dimension rather completely in order to sense the basic composition of your Earth experience and why many of you have thought of it as a limitation or a restriction.

The 3rd dimension vibrates rather slowly, there is a pulse or a beat, a divine rhythm if you will which breathes in and breathes out at only about 1/10th of the rate of the Source level. The beat then is much slower. Now, we are talking here within physical existence which has a sequential flow - time and space are present or seem to be. Time and space are simply the magnification process within the dimensions and each dimension up through the 6th deals with it in a little different manner.

Beyond the 6th dimension there is a different "process" that is not sequential, it has no time or space. Within the 3rd dimension the beat, the rhythm is so slow that it freezes divine activity rather like taking a picture freezes motion and then you can put it back together. You know that's the way early motion pictures were made - taking a series of pictures and then flipping them rapidly so they seemed to move.

If you take a picture, the movement can be studied because it seems frozen, you can look at that movement, you magnify that movement to get an opportunity to look at that movement - that literally is the purpose of the 3rd dimension for you as a divine being.

The movement represents the creative process or you could say that the 3rd dimension is a Creator's How-To-Do-It Kit that has been slowed down 10-fold so you can take it all apart, study each part of it and then put it back together so that you can see that you have understood how to do so. Of course the goal is to have it work when you put it together again.

You, then, are taking your unlimitedness apart on the Earth plane, looking at it in a magnified manner through what is called a mirroring process - life mirrors to you all of what you are seeking to understand about it. You will hear me, in many ways, and as often as possible talking about mirroring because it is a key to understanding the creative process, to understanding yourself and to understanding of others. The 3rd dimension then is the structure of the slowed down creative flow that allows you to see through a mirroring process all of creation. Far from being a limitation, physical existence lays it out, from every point of view, all you have to do is to be conscious enough to see the complete layout. I often like to use the example of a very busy freeway system. Let us use Los Angeles as a prime example, although any large city in the world could be used as an example.

If you look at the freeway system from an objective point of view from above it at any time of the day or night you will see a particular pattern of flow, each vehicle represents a part of that creative flow. The flow itself and the way that it is moving can tell us a great deal but each component within the flow, each vehicle, the way it looks, the way it sounds, the way it relates to every other vehicle is also an important key as we study creatively this vehicular flow on the busy freeway system.

You see, there is never an accident within creation. Through this synchronicity of the freeway system we can learn much about humanity feeling stuck and caught and crowded in a 3rd dimensional flow, feeling there isn't enough room for all units, or aspects of consciousness, that some must wait, that they are crowded out by the sheer volume of the flow. Now this is not true but the key to understanding it lies beyond the 3rd dimension so we will get to that a little later but we can see a certain "style" of flow within the 3rd dimension and if you keep adding to it eventually you get, just as the traffic in Los Angeles has gotten, to a point where the flow moves with less and less efficiency and more and more clogging or slowing down results. You can see then that the freeway structure has been overloaded without taking into consideration other flow systems that can clear out the problems that have been erroneously allowed to creep into the system.

EXERCISE: See yourself as a car on a busy freeway. What alternatives are there? What options do you have so that you feel comfortable in the traffic flow? Create that now.

The 4th dimension equals the **_Flow_** and there is a part of this flow which equates to the Astral level but only from one point of view. The flow could be considered to be a river, a river which flows smoothly and evenly, and, my friends - very deeply. Sometimes the 3rd dimension could be considered a flow but it has no depth to that flow, only the 4th dimension penetrates deeply as it flows and it is this deep penetrative content of the 4th dimension which makes it the key to your multi-dimensional potentiality.

Now, if you have reached a point in your life where perhaps the city has become too much for you, you say to yourself, "I don't want to live in this city anymore," and you move either next to the ocean or to a body of water, it may simply be a mountain stream, it may be a large lake that has movement, it will allow you to begin to sense movement again as perhaps in the large city it didn't seem possible. This is the basis for many of you leaving certain areas, going into other areas because you can't sense any flow in your life. You're looking for a connection or a flow into a connection. Perhaps we could put it that way.

Now, certainly the 4th dimension will flow anything that enters it so all aspects or parts of who you are can benefit from the use of this 4th dimension. Certainly your physical structure will benefit from it and that's why swimming is so valuable to many of you. It allows you to literally sense physically a movement, a flow that is used in yet a 3rd dimensional format meaning that your physical body may still be using the 3rd dimension but through entering a body of water, a lake, a stream, an ocean and swimming within it, it begins to build a bridge, get a glimpse of or understand that there is a means, another structure that will allow a fuller movement physically.

For many of you, the key to creating a clearer physical life is to glimpse that that is possible in a creative manner. In other words, many times you must prove to your subconscious mind by which you create your life that it is possible to move freely, to flow your life.

I would say that for all of you now, and this is being written in August of 1988, some sort of physical activity that equates to flow will be very helpful. Swimming, waterskiing, walking, jogging, running, bicycle riding, something where there is movement, certainly dancing, the Eastern disciplines of Tai Chi or Yoga. Something that shows a creative <u>movement</u> on the physical level can be very helpful. Now that includes the assistance of your physical body in removing certain stuck energy patterns which it is holding. These can be done through a number of energy methods. Types of body and etheric work which allow the physical structure to become clearer is also helpful. You see, the synchronicity, my friends, is that your 3rd dimensional focus can access a flow potential which is that 4th dimension. We will seek to discover together ways by which that can be done.

EXERCISE: See yourself in a row boat floating on a beautiful river. You are able to move easily on the river. You have the stability system built into your boat so even if a storm comes up you are very stable and moving in the flow. Create that visualization now.

Thus we see that through the 4th dimension consciousness can access divine understanding through movement, the 4th dimension is literally the movement of consciousness on any level, in any situation.

The 5th dimension is the structural blueprinting system on any level. Many of you have seen this 5th dimension clairvoyantly and it always contains geometric shapes. There may be large crystals seen, the colors are magnificent, one shape flowing into another and seen through the beautiful colors that interlock the structural geometry of creation. The 5th dimension I have called _**structure**_ but perhaps we may define it even more clearly as "ideal" structure or the building blocks by which creation takes place. They are organized, put together in a manner that is uniquely appropriate for the Earth within the 5th dimension. Many times we could say that the 5th dimension is very compatible with the mental body and the 4th dimension very compatible with the emotional body. The 5th dimension then shows an orderly and organized building block connection, it has a logical process and a conceptual overview which makes available the creative potential for physical existence.

One needs to bridge all dimensions to understand the full use of each dimension because they are not meant to be used in an isolated manner. To do so is a distortion. If you came to the Earth, for example, and saw a house which was only a bathroom, you would get a distorted glimpse of what type of life was lived on the Earth. You need to put one structure into a larger picture in order to see its use completely as a part of divine order.

It seems to me, Vywamus, that this type of information is exactly what humanity needs in order to see beyond the confusion of what has been "structured" on the Earth in the erroneous belief that it is part of the ideal that is being sought on the Earth. The process is redefining reality on your Earth. The process being the divine plan. A breaking down of the old is absolutely essential in order to bring in the divine order which is sought here. Some will hold onto the old in the erroneous perception that it is "needed." One must be clear enough to see beyond illusion, to release old patterns of behaviour, to allow change, to be secure enough to communicate until change brings you the clearer Earth which has now been born.

The use of the 5th dimension is essential because within it is the concept, the divine order, the divine blueprinting system that is sought now.

EXERCISE: See yourself at the gateway of a city of crystals. There are crystals in all shapes and sizes and colors. Go down into the city, walk among the crystals, see what comes up for you as you do so.

Dimension 6 is the *ideal*. I have given some

material in the past about the 6th dimension but I am going to go deeper into it now. I have said that the 5th dimension contains the divine blueprinting system and that is true. The concept has been allowed to come together into a planned structure but before, if you will, entering that structure it is stored within the 6th dimension. Now that may seem rather difficult at first to comprehend but it is really very simple and simplicity, it seems to me, has been difficult for humanity to comprehend. If its simple, humanity generally wants to know why is it that simple? What's the catch? What is being hidden? Simplicity is really not yet understood so connecting physical existence to a high level is the level of simplicity that I will now call the 6th dimension.

We could call the ideal blueprint complete understanding. We could call it the complete qualities as they seek to work out in physical existence. Another way of saying, although we have not yet gotten to the 9th dimension, is that it reflects from the basic or the core level, which the 9th dimension represents. This basic level of existence that can then be used as a key to creating clearly on the physical level is then reflected into the 6th dimension and inspires more directly the physical. There are many of us, your teachers, in fact about 70% of us, function on that level or put our main energy into that 6th dimensional level. So you have a stepped down process from that remote or 9th dimensional understanding to use in your life. That is what we, the teachers, are literally, a stepping down process for physical existence to learn from, to understand and to, in many cases, emulate. We stimulate then the basic Source level responses that stimulate responses within the 6th dimension so that they are not as difficult for you in physical existence to relate to and to understand.

Certainly we could say there is a basic galactic connection here. I would equate both the 6th and 7th dimension to the galactic core but the galactic core inputs into the 6th dimension in a way which allows you on the Earth to begin a more complete usage of the dimensions. It is important to understand divine movement not in opposition to, but in addition to, physical movement.

You understand physical movement. There is a stepping forward of the physical structure. Divine movement is a lightening perspective. As you move forward physically the communicative link with all the divine structures or dimensions that you "live in" allows you to <u>understand</u> 6th dimensional input more clearly so that the light within you reflects from the 9th dimension, flowing through the 8th, 7th and a relay where the energy is re-stimulated in the 6th dimension so that it can flow directly into the 1st, 2nd, 3rd, 4th, 5th, and through the rest of the 6th dimension.

Thus you could say that the 6th dimension is the electrical circuitry system that makes sure that there is enough divine current so that it meets all of the structures needs, all of the dimensional structures needs. The circuitry system is a part of the 5th dimension but the electrical flow of it is generated from the 6th dimension, stimulates the 4th which is the flow and allows the 5th to contact that whole blueprinting system and then access the 3rd dimensions magnification system in order to stimulate the 1st dimension completion of a level of understanding and the beginning of the next level which is the 2nd dimensional contact.

EXERCISE: See a golden ball. Place that golden ball within your heart area and allow it to expand and expand and expand. You know that this golden ball is electrical in nature. See what occurs for you physically, emotionally, mentally and spiritually through this golden ball expansion.

Between the 6th and the 7th dimension there is a corridor, you really call that corridor a turnaround point for the inner and the outer experience. As you go to sleep each night you travel in the 7th dimension in order to reach the inner experience that you have. Now the inner experience can contain the 3rd, the 4th, the 5th and the 6th dimension but not the same view of them. A good example would be going to school as a student and you view life in the school as a student, that is the outer experience. When you return to the school later as a visitor, you are no longer a student, you are still able to view the process that is used at the school but you are no longer as personally involved with it. You have a certain objectivity and this would be looking at the dimensions from the inner point of view. You are able to be more objective in an experiential sense, not only in a mental or a conceptual sense so that your 7th dimension is literally a corridor which allows you to reframe the way you experience the dimensional structures. Now this is very valuable and we will get into it quite comprehensively a little later in this dimensional excursion. For now, let us say the 7th dimension equals _**a turnaround point**_ which allows experiential objectivity.

The 8th dimension is an area which contains all potentiality. It unites together the concept which sourceness is seeking to explore, to understand and perhaps the word _**"color laboratory"**_ might apply here, recognizing that colors are energy and a complete spectrum of energy would be all potentialities. What we have within the 8th dimension is a laboratory where potentialities are tried out, are experimented with to see how to expand their usage, to add certain creative variables which will allow the Source to expand its understanding in any particular desirable area.

In other material I have talked about a Cosmic Day. It is a conceptual framework by which the Source may completely explore a particular theme. This Cosmic Day which is four billion, three hundred million of your earth years, has a theme of courage.

Now, let us say that you set up a cosmic laboratory somewhere in the ethers. That is what the 8th dimension is doing. In as many ways as we can all of us who make up the Source are creatively exploring courage on this Cosmic Day, from every point of view, in every way but the ideas coming from the co-creator level in the 9th dimension are first tried out in this 8th dimensional laboratory. This lab puts together certain possibilities to see how compatible they are and how well they will allow the subject being explored to flow creatively and to expand.

The goal of creation is expansion of whatever theme is being explored. Now that is not the full purpose of creation, I have stated over and over that I believe the full purpose of creation is simply a joyous expression, a loving exercise in creativity but within this overall purpose there are certain themes, certain areas of exploration and the goal is to explore those themes, those areas as completely and as expansively as possible.

Literally, the goal of creation is expansion of anything and everything. Thus in the 8th dimension one of the most important attributes of it is its expanding qualities. If we had 9 rubber bands, each one representing a dimension the most expansive, the one with the most elasticity in it is the 8th dimension because the planners, those representatives of the co-creators, will check out the possibilities, try to push it to the limit in the 8th dimension, to see the potentialities in every area, building in what one might call a "fail safe" method by doing so.

In other words, you set up stress testing in such a laboratory knowing that if you test it for 10 times the stress that you think will be present in the normal usage that you've built in a fail safe system. If it works at 10 times the expected stress, certainly it will work at the normal stress.

Now, in theory this is a very good system, in actuality it doesn't always work out that way. Thus many Cosmic Days are not concluded. They work for a while and then they do not work well. They are then reframed, concluded rather suddenly. It would be like reading to page fifty in a volume that has two hundred pages, deciding there wasn't any point in going on and reading the rest. This might be because; one, the story is boring, two, you can't understand it and so why get further involved, third, it isn't really flowing for you. So for whatever reason you decide to close the book. The closing of the book is the early termination of that Cosmic Day.

Now when that occurs the 8th dimension is always very busy because those in charge want to know -"alright, why didn't this work?" and so it goes back to the laboratory to see why it didn't work. In one sense the 8th dimension contains many Cosmic Days that are playing out in a laboratory to see where they actually would have gone if they had been allowed to play out. There are literally thousands of them playing out in the 8th dimension. It is a fascinating place to visit and if you ask me I will be glad to set up some tours for you to help you get into some of those exotic experiences which you would have been in anyway if it had been decided to allow them to play out in the full fledged creative role playing that we are all in now.

It would be the difference between what the movies do, using miniatures, and sets and the full blown experience on a larger level. I'm sure that many of you know that the movies use small sets to depict something, an earthquake or a destructive event, or an event that is looking at space and certain planets in space. In your science fiction movies they use miniature sets to depict the full blown event. Thus, in the 8th dimension, these miniaturized Cosmic Days if you will, are fulfilling their destiny, playing out and it is very important that they be allowed to do so.

One thing that occurred at the end of July, 1988 that I took into consideration when I said that the year since the Harmonic Convergence was a time of adjustment, a time of getting used to a new energy formatting here on the Earth and that by the end of July I felt, and still feel, that humanity and the Earth itself would be beginning to see more clearly in how to use this new Earth, this new creative opportunity on the Earth now. One reason then, was there were no fewer than 10 Cosmic

Day experiences that were being concluded, ones that had been interrupted, pulled back from the larger picture, been miniaturized and placed in a sequencing format. It is necessary to see that that is important. At the Source level there is not time and space as you know it but in this 8th dimensional laboratory it is simulated within these miniature experiences. The purpose of that is to include physical existence in the resolution. It is very important that physical existence benefit from the resolution of these experiences. This was realized by the co-creators long ago, the reason being again the nature of the dimensions and the 3rd dimension particularly, the magnified process benefits from finishing up what has been started in a larger sense, then pulled back and miniaturized in order to be completed.

When I saw 10 Cosmic Days finishing up within a few sequential days of one another from July 25, 1988 to August 10, 1988 I knew what an important time this was for your Earth as well as for the whole cosmos. In point in fact, I have used this 8th dimensional laboratory in a predictive way successfully over and over again. I can pretty much tell by the theme of what is being finished up in the laboratory that a clearer of resolution of that theme will begin to be expressed on your Earth as that experience finishes up.

Let us say, in your life, that you have decided to become an engineer and you are going to school studying many things. Now you need in a certain sequence the mathematics, the science, the word skills, the logic. Many, courses are needed to keep building on your understanding in order to become that engineer, to be ready to utilize your understanding or the beginning of it truly in an actual job. But let us say that you are in beginning calculus and your teacher leaves for one reason or another and there is not another teacher available so beginning calculus which you've just gotten into is discontinued and they tell you that it won't be available for a while - you will have to pick the credit up later.

Now in the meantime you are studying other subjects but some of them build from your understanding of this subject of beginning calculus which you now do not have, cannot take. There gets to be a gap then in the system - let us be really far out and say that another subject also is pulled back because of the unavailability of a teacher. Now you have two gaps, you go ahead with your studies and you may not at the time realize that the gaps are there but they are. And let us continue to be far out and say that it is two years before you can get your beginning calculus and the other subject. Now you can't really get very far without those two subjects, there is no way to balance your understanding for the desired career and it is more in the area of purposes that this affects you on the Earth, not so much the living your life in a general sense but as you focus into the purpose area there gets to be gaps in the putting together or integrating your sense of purpose as a soul. Your soul always has a rather intricate purpose, it's never one thing, it's a combination and the flow. It is never just one event, or one purpose. However in our example if there are areas that for one reason or another are a foundation you need for your understanding and you haven't allowed them to be a part of your experience then on the cosmic level a finishing up of one of these miniaturized Cosmic Days will help you fill in the gaps. It becomes a cosmic substitute for the physical experience.

What I'm telling you is that the plan, the cosmic plan allows growth and learning from every point of view and if, because you have not yet recognized your own unlimitedness, you limit your foundation in discovering your purpose in any way, then there are cosmic events that directly link to you and allow a resolution to come into your life cosmically. Now, what would occur in our example is that if that cosmic miniaturized day concluded and you were still in school suddenly a very good teacher or tutor would appear and very easily you would get caught up in the areas that were not yet - or had not yet been available to you. You may not realize or recognize that as a cosmic resolution but it is. You will feel lighter, there will be, let us say, in our example a very good relationship with the tutor and a very easy resolution of what had been a problem because the 8th dimensional input is directly assisting you to allow the foundation to become clearer.

Now what I wish to do in this material is to give you the 10 Cosmic Days that had been miniaturized, the dates that they completed and what their theme was. By knowing these you may be able to look at your own personal life, at the lives of your friends and at the Earth to see how this cosmic resolution has aided you. Now one cannot expect everything to clear in a particular area for you from one miniaturized cosmic resolution. The reason is that other areas feed into this area and it depends upon how you created your experience as to how helpful this resolution is for you. But if you think about 10 Cosmic Days, even though they are miniturized completing in such a short sequential period on the Earth then you know indeed that it is making available a whole new way of viewing existence.

Alright, let me give those to you now:

#	DATE	THEME
1	July 25, 1988	Unlimited Energy
2	July 26, 1988	Parallels of Love
3	July 26, 1988	Joyous Beginnings
4	July 28, 1988	Balancing of Oppositions
5	July 30, 1988	Integration
6	July 31, 1988	Unlimited Communication
7	August 3, 1988	Surrender to the Plan
8	August 6, 1988	Sacrifice
9	August 7, 1988	Unconditional Love
10	August 10, 1988	Joyous Movement

Now, remember, all of these 10 themes represent cosmic experiences that were pulled back because they were not working, often, most importantly, on the physical level. So they were discontinued from the larger perspective, put into a miniature state and allowed to work out. What I mean by their completion is they have worked out successfully so that the theme was explored completely and a satisfactory resolution was made. Now, many of these themes were explored over and over again in the miniturized state and seemed to be very blocked. A good example of that would be the number 9 - Unconditional Love. Finally there was a satisfactory conclusion, the miniaturization showed a positive resolution, an exploration of unconditional love from every point of view so that it was entirely satisfactory. Now you can see that this resolution is extremely important and that on the level of the 8th dimension there is in an <u>experiential sense of a good resolution of these areas.</u>

Now, because of the unlimited nature of existence certainly one could turn around and "plant" a new cosmic experience in each of these areas and go on from that point to the next but the fact that each of these cosmic experiences were pulled back and not completed has affected existence ever since. It's again like starting the course and then not being able to finish it - that's what the 8th dimensional laboratory is working out, all possibilities working out there and then we can use the strengths that are developed there - the doorway opens and we can then creatively learn to access what is stored there. This is probably one of the most important pieces of information you are ever going to receive on any level. It is important to recognize that the Source in its clear sense of responsibility would never just begin something without completing it in one way or another and you can benefit personally from what is being learned or gained cosmically here.

To say that I will be talking about this 8th dimension more is probably an understatement because we are going to be emphasizing now how to use it and how to let its light enlighten you on the physical plane.

EXERCISE: See yourself surrounded by 10 doors and choose from the 10 Cosmic Days that I've given you 1 that you would like to explore. So write on one of the doors, from the list given, the words of the theme, i.e., if you choose "Unconditional Love" then write that on your doorway. Then see yourself entering an environment where unconditional love has been explored and brought to a satisfactory resolution, not concluded permanently, but brought to a level or resolution where it works for everyone. That's the important clue there - that it works for everyone. Go through the door and see what you get in a experiential way. The goal will be to see an experience where unconditional love is working for everyone. Thus, in whatever theme that you choose, that you can note what sort of an effect comes into being through the conclusion of a particular cosmic experience in that area.

The 9th dimension is literally the Source's overall viewing level and the home territory of the co-creator levels, whether it is a fully realized co-creator or for each of you the part of you that already functions on that level. You might look at it this way - you can see a flat plane and on it sits an unlimited number of buckets. Now some of the buckets are half full, some are a quarter full, some just have a little in them and some - a few - are full. Now you can visualize them full of anything you want, stars, water, anything. But the ones that are full - and there aren't too many of them, are the fully realized co-creator's on the 9th dimension. There are many buckets that just have a little in them, don't they? For many of you, you are in the process of filling your bucket with the star potential and placing it into that fully realized co-creator level that I am calling the 9th dimension.

Now, this 9th dimension certainly interacts with all of the dimensions and it is the administrator, if you will, of all of the dimensions. It is also the _"think tank"_ for the co-creator level where the conception of existence takes place and that is the experiential side of existence. Keep in mind that when I am talking about dimensions, I am talking about a framework for activity. Your divine beingness lies much beyond any sort of a dimensional structure, your divine beingness transcends any sort of a dimensional structure but here we are talking about, the divine structural support system which allows consciousness to explore and expand its potential through the service mode that it chooses and that it allows to grow and to expand.

Certainly the 9th dimension is for all of you that basic point of Creator contact. Your contact with the Creator goes through the structural system into what you call the Source itself. The Source can be contacted from many points of view because the beingness permeates everything, thus your contact with Source may be through a beautiful gentle butterfly or a small fawn in the forest or a beautiful flower or a loving contact with another human being. It is not always a 9th dimensional experience but the basic point of contact with evolution, with a growing awareness comes from the 9th dimension. The spiral begins here, the growth is implemented here, the discovery process is born on the 9th dimension. One discovers the means to transcend, to release, to allow, to serve in many, many ways but it is through this 9th dimensional contact that one can sense the joyous allowingness of a Source relationship.

By understanding how to contact the 9th dimension, your emotional body can feel that support that it is looking for and through that contact will allow a mirroring into physical existence of the support system you are seeking. Thus, it is very worthwhile to continue to explore with me within these pages how to contact and utilize the 9th dimension as completely and comprehensively as you can. There is a sense then of transcendence as you allow that dimensional contact to be made. Let's do together the following exercise:

EXERCISE: See yourself sitting at the top of a mountain. Now you are very comfortable, it is a wide open space, its neither too hot or too cold and you're sitting there very comfortably at the very peak of this mountain. Allow yourself to experience it. What comes into your awareness as you experience the top of the mountain? Now if you begin to feel cold or some other emotion which is resistive comes in then clear that out, follow that and find out what its attached to. Perhaps you froze to death on the top of a mountain - be clear in your subconscious association with the top of the mountain experience, clear it out and when you are clear then go back again to the top of the mountain, sit there my friends and receive - see what comes into you.

Now this is an exercise that is meant to be done progressively. Make a realization at the top of your mountain then follow that realization to the next step in your greater understanding of who you are and then go back to the top of your mountain. I could give you an example here: perhaps as you are sitting on the top of your mountain you see a golden door - well go within the golden door if that's what you want to do - open the golden door, go within, experience and learn from that contact - then when you feel you've learned as much as you can - go back again and sit at the top of the mountain and see what experience comes to you then. You can keep using the top of the mountain experience to contact opportunities that are truly being sent to you from the 9th dimension.

CHAPTER 2

YOUR FOUR BODIES IN THE DIMENSIONS

Your four body system is learning to flow, to live within all dimensions. On the inner planes or during your sleep period on the outer planes you are learning to utilize an integrated viewpoint of all dimensional structure. Ascension - the point where you are able to leave the physical - is also the point where you have integrated into most dimensional opportunities. Certainly you will continue, after the ascension process, to understand dimensions and how to use them more clearly but you could say the fundamentals will have been learned or understood and thus after ascension you need not take courses or exist within a physical structure which is designed to teach you multi-dimensional expression.

Now you probably have not thought about the physical structure as a vehicle for teaching multi-dimensional expression but it was designed expressly to do that. Now in the 3rd dimension which I have equated to a magnification process there is an opportunity because of this magnification to view or get acquainted with each dimension and your use of it within the four body system. That is the difference between the inner and the outer experience. The inner experience flows so easily that if you have any "bugs" in the system or if you have not understood a certain aspect of creativity completely by the time you try to figure it out you've flowed beyond that point into another dimensional format.

Thus the Creator has designed a structure which will allow a mirroring of any particular dimensional inconsistencies, gaps, avoidance patterns, and what one might call doubling-up in ability to use the ideal blueprinting grid system which your soul has designed specifically for use in your life. You could say the dimensions are a grid system in which you dance creatively and the dance needs to be balanced, taking in all points of the grid system for use in your life.

If you live in a house and there is a room that you never use you are not taking advantage of an opportunity to access the strengths of what that room represents thus life mirrors to you certain inconsistencies when the dimensional format is not well adjusted, well integrated. We are going to explore in this dimensional journey many, many ways of seeing how you function dimensionally so that you can find any inconsistencies which you may have and learn to let go of such inconsistencies and bring your use of the dimensions into a more integrated focus.

Your Earth is approaching the 4th dimension. Now this is true and yet it isn't true as I have stated several times - the positive part of that statement is that everything will flow more easily and communication will be more consistent and reach deeper levels of understanding in a progressive manner, this has already begun on your Earth in this month of August, 1988. Certainly it is but the beginning of a freer flow of communication and there will be "seeming" set backs for a while which are not set backs but are negotiation tactics in order to find a path which is acceptable to those within the communication link.

Let us say that several of you, for example, are driving down a highway. Now your goal is to reach a particular city and you are driving there. And you have several alternative routes to get there. You may go the interstate freeway or you can take a more picturesque winding road which takes a little longer or there is a third alternative that rather combines both, it doesn't take as long as the second one but it is more picturesque than the first alternative. Can you see that first, through communication, decisions on literally how to approach the goal or the use of the dimensional gridwork must be made. Therefore, when working with a group and utilizing the group process communicatively you can, many times, bypass individual resistances by allowing the group consensus to be the motivator which moves the communicative link forward and flows it interdimensionally.

Now of course on your Earth these national or individual differences have in your past created blocks where each nation or individual felt isolated, felt "picked upon" or the victim of certain aggressive potentialities from other nations or individuals. This particular block within humanity is not as strong in the mass consciousness as it was and I attribute it directly to the raising of consciousness on the planet - to each of you releasing certain deep resistant areas and to helping your friends to do so too. I would encourage you to keep looking for - through communication - the clearer understanding of yourselves, of your nations, of humanity and of the whole Earth.

Communication is the key. As we discuss it in a dimensional focus we begin to see that it is literally the "highway system" of your New Age and you make choices in how to negotiate the system.

You probably realize as you read this that you have a four body system - a physical, emotional, mental and spiritual body or focus which is a focus of conscious awareness, a unique perspective which inputs to your own personal life and to the planetary life. It also inputs to humanity and to those relationships and groups of which you are a part. We could say you speak one language physically, another language emotionally, a third one mentally and yet the fourth one or perhaps the overall one - spiritually.

Each body of your four body system relates to the grid or dimensional structure differently. Each body has an affinity for certain dimensions and does not recognize as completely other dimensions it has perhaps not explored within your physical life. Although certain of your bodies have used some of the dimensions they still do not understand them clearly.

It would be like saying your emotional body had studied calculus but it certainly didn't understand what calculus is and how to use it within its emotional perspective. Now, that brings up an interesting point - is your emotional body supposed to relate to calculus or something equally "foreign" to its experience? My reply to that is not in the way that, in our example, your mental body relates to calculus. But your emotional body must acknowledge within the dimensional grid system that it can contact calculus as a dimensional point or focus. This will trigger a response into the life which integrates certain opportunities and opens up possibilities.

If your emotional body says to you "I won't enter the classroom where calculus is being taught," then it is blocking your mental body's learning tool, which, in our example, is calculus. Again, I am not saying that calculus is necessary for everyone, it is simply an example of each body's way of relating to certain learning or dimensional grid system opportunities which will become a strength in that particular area.

You could say that each of your four bodies becomes an expert in its own area, the area where it is uniquely compatible within the grid system and then it will allow an interchange with the other bodies from that point of view which, if the other bodies reciprocate or allow it, brings to that point of awareness an integration.

What I am saying is within any group the individuals of that group (and I am now calling your four body system a group) and the group can use the expertise of each member. The group can learn how to utilize and be a part of a specific area of the dimensional grid system by an <u>allowing</u> and <u>reciprocal</u> exchange from each dimensional focus.

Let us say that dimensions 3, 4, 5 and 6 are four islands. Now in our example your physical body is standing in the 3rd dimension, the emotional body in the 4th dimension, the mental body in the 5th dimension and the spiritual body in the 6th dimension. Each of your bodies has a particular affinity for the dimensions that I have just given which does not mean that that is the only place they function, but it means that their strengths are utilized very well from the grid system brought through your physical planet Earth and individualized through your soul. So your soul has used the Creator's physicalized grid system for the Earth to give your four body system a point of contact within physicality where it can be "at home." That doesn't, of course, mean that it is its

43

home but it is a "comfort zone."

Now, going back to our example of the four islands what we are seeking to do in this volume is to show you the choices that you have made about the use of these four dimensions in physical existence.

Visualize then or draw the following on a piece of paper: you can personify each of your bodies as a person. Draw the four islands placing on the left your island which is the 3rd dimension with your physical body then next to it the 4th dimension with your emotional body and then moving further to the right an island with the 5th dimension and your mental body on the far right an island with your 6th dimension, which you could call the spiritual body.

Now if you've drawn these on a piece of paper look at the diagram and it will show you one way to use this representation of the dimensional grid system. You will note that what we now need is a connection between the dimensions and you can draw bridges to each dimension from each other dimension. Then complete the circle having the flow come back to the original dimension. Thus you have a group of interconnecting circles of energy. Visualize and feel this energy connecting these dimensions that you have drawn.

In this section we are going to explore extensively ways of seeing how you are currently relating in a four body sense to the dimensions. I would suggest that you try all of the exercises, and of course some of them will "speak" to you more clearly than others. After trying <u>all</u> of the exercises then go back and repeat the ones that seemed especially helpful. If some exercises don't speak to you at all, you may, at a later time want to try those again also because sometimes if a particular body or part of you is not ready to acknowledge or confront an exercise it can turn off the possibility of learning from it.

For others of you, you may have already integrated part of an exercise goal within your life and if you recognize that is true then simply proceed to the next exercise. However, I would say that almost all these exercises can be used by most of you and will help you both to understand what the dimensions are and then provide a choice about how to use the dimensions.

EXERCISE: See or know (one does not have to be visual to use these exercises - your knowingness or imagination can assist you in doing that) your emotional body standing on the island which represents the 4th dimension. Have your emotional body, which you are visualizing now as a person, look at the island and describe it to you. Is it lush and green? Is it a desert? Is the sun shining? Is it raining? Is the wind blowing? Is there a city there? Are there people? Are there animals? Try to be as specific as possible. Now you will probably find with your emotional body that you get a feeling about the island and then your four body system can tell you about the island.

This is the goal. Your emotional body experiences or you've asked it to. Your mental, spiritual and yes, your physical bodies can then share in describing the island.

Spend at least 15 minutes with this experience. Now some of you, although the emotional body has a natural affinity for the 4th dimension, have not used that 4th dimension emotionally - now isn't that interesting?

So in this first exercise it is very important that you spend enough time, maybe several days, getting acquainted emotionally with this island. Study the material I have given about the 4th dimension with your mental body; ask your spiritual body through your soul to bring in a perspective of it also; ask your physical body what it is receiving through the feeling nature or the association with the emotional body as you get acquainted with this 4th dimensional point of view that we have called an island. The goal of this particular exercise is to have your emotional body perceive the structure, the layout if you will, of the 4th dimension. It is one of the most important exercises you can do to help your growing awareness.

One thing that makes it so important is the Earth's growing awareness of the 4th dimension. You have heard over and over the

Earth is moving into the 4th dimension - what that simply means is that there is a focus, a conscious awareness of how to use the 4th dimension in a growing and expanding manner now on the Earth.

I have suggested that you spend 15 minutes on this exercise but if you really want to get the full benefit of it, why don't you imagine or visualize for 24 hours, that your daily experience is 4th dimensional. Ask your spiritual knowingness, ask your mental body, ask your physical body - pretend or imagine that you've suddenly been transported from 75 to 100 years into your future. What would conditions be like then?

First of all transportation will flow physically over your planet in a way that you have yet to experience. In my opinion, many of you will be easily teleported within your body of light vehicle. In the magnification process of the 3rd dimension, it is literally almost impossible to flow the body of light in a consistent and therefore focused manner. The light spectrum of the 3rd dimension is so magnified that it breaks up the flow, therefore one must move into the 4th dimension, the flow potential of the dimensional structure in order to move as light. That means that your physical body must be willing to allow or become acquainted with the use of the 4th dimension.

Visualize then, as completely as you can, a sort of a life where things flow easily, where physicality is more flowing. We've stated that

47

communication will be fuller, will be more complete. We've stated that you will be able to move physically much more easily and that includes, my friends, the physical activity that you enjoy doing - walking, running, dancing, jogging, exercising in any way - swimming, sports. All of these things will flow easier within the 4th dimension. New sports also will be created.

Certainly one of the great benefits will be the communicative link within the galactic quadrant within which you now live. You will get to know your neighbors, my friends, those that are now able to use the 4th dimension, and I'm going to give you here a piece of information which may seem strange to you but if you think about it I think you can understand it. Your 3rd dimensional Earth which we've equated to an island in the 3rd dimension has already a 4th dimension equivalency - there is another island there and its potential, its structure is already developed. Also, on that Earth, if you will, there are beings which exist, live, and have a certain awareness level that is a little more complete than yours.

We are talking about a alternate reality as far as your Earth is concerned. Now there are many, many, many ways to talk about alternate realities and this dimensional book is a primer or beginning manual for you to understand them in a way that can show what they really are rather than something that seems too difficult to comprehend.

So continuing to simplify the process then we could say that there is an Earth or a part of the Earth now, that is focused in the 3rd dimension, there is an Earth or a part of an Earth that is focused in the 4th dimension, there is an Earth or a part of an Earth which is focused in the 5th dimension and a part of an Earth that is focused in the 6th dimension. Now whether you are an individual person or a planet what you are trying to do is unite your conscious understanding of all perspectives so that the ultimate reality of the Earth within the 4th dimension is simply a part of the overall dimensional structure of the Earth which is the next focus of attention in the integrational process of the planet which we call the Earth.

It is really a simple process, there is always a supportive structure given by our Creator for us to explore every aspect of consciousness. Thus your Earth is moving into the 4th dimension or exploring this island that we have placed your emotional body on. Thus, my friends, the emotional perspective of the Earth also is simply a process of looking at or expressing an ever clearer creative flow that gathers up and integrates your potential which is included in the Earth's potential and allows evolution to take place.

Therefore, in this first exercise, when exploring this 4th dimension as this island adventure as clearly as possible add the quality of your imagination to it so that you can get "far-out." This allows you to begin to sense what the 4th dimension is all about. Don't be afraid to stretch in your imagination 4th dimensionally. That's what the 4th dimension is all about - it stretches very easily. So allow yourself to stretch through your imagination. For a little while tell your mental body to put on hold, if you will, the logical process. Now, not the conceptual or the higher mental, keep that one on tap but the way that you have used or haven't used the 4th dimension will seem to you to be the logical process. Put that on hold now as you imagine the use of it. For those of you who consider yourself to be very mental, you think about life a lot, you have had a tendency perhaps to bury emotional responses as not appropriate, as making life more difficult, as an unnecessary and unwelcome point of view. Your mental body needs the 4th dimension as given to you through your emotional perspective. That doesn't mean that the mental body can't cross over to this island itself, it can, but its host or the one that will welcome it, is ideally the emotional body.

Now your emotional body will certainly explore the other islands also but its home base within the ideal grid system is the 4th dimension. Now the reason I've given this exercise first is, for many of you, your emotional body is not well acquainted with the 4th dimension. Now in a volume such as this there are perhaps 40% of you where it is well acquainted but the other 60% are not acquainted emotionally with the 4th dimension and because of that this exercise, done over and over, done whenever you have a few moments of envisioning a life with a lot of flow and all of the other things that you understand and assimilate about the 4th dimension will help you to get the ideal emotionally of how to use it.

Certainly it is necessary to have some sort of a clearing system, in my opinion, to help each aspect of yourself release old blocks. If you do not currently have a clearing system I refer you to other material within the Foundation in regard to clearing blocks that are affecting you subconsciously. You can obtain a catalog from the Foundation Headquarters and you will see other books and other booklets and other informational papers which can help you to understand more fully what areas you have blocks within. There are also Personal Intensives done in the Youngtown, Arizona headquarters where I, Vywamus, go deeply into those blocks which I see within you to help you release them, move beyond those old patterns, move beyond the usage of the dimensional structure in the old way that may not have been serving you well, allowing you to contact those ideal usages that are part of your soul's blueprinting system and part of its purpose on the Earth.

One thing that can help you in the exploration of the 4th dimensional possibilities on the Earth is to unite with the Earth perspective as much as you can. Remember, the Earth also is seeking to explore a new way of looking at the 4th dimension. It is getting acquainted or bridging to that part of itself which is centered in the 4th dimension.

Seeing the Earth 4th dimensionally can be helpful to you as well as helpful to the Earth. Can you see that a 4th dimensional Earth will be clear of pollution because pollution is literally a result of a magnification process in the 3rd dimension that then gets stuck and caught and has no way to release from that perspective. It needs the 4th dimensional flow to "blow it out." So visualizing all parts of your Earth, the streams, the rivers, the oceans, the forests, the trees, the mountains, the cities, the soil itself, the flowers, the mineral kingdom itself, as releasing the stored up pollution which is just a 3rd dimensional stuck point of view, is like cleaning house.

It's time for your Earth to clean house by releasing the 3rd dimensional debris which has accumulated within it. That has stressed the Earth, the heating up process or the fractionalizing of the atmosphere is coming about through the stress patterns of not yet accessing the flow of the 4th dimension. The cleansing quality of the 4th dimension is going to be evident in the last few years of this century. It will not always be understood but if you can look at it as a house cleaning, as a means to re-establish a contact point with that 4th dimensional Earth which already exists, which shines there for you, then it will be easier to comprehend what is going on.

In our anology of the islands that correspond to dimensions the bridging from the 3rd dimension to the 4th dimensional island must be cleared. Not only must the planet flow more clearly but there are still a few remaining rather large blocks in the approach to the 4th dimension. If we see a bridge with about eight-tenths of it now cleared but the final two-tenths still blocked, all piled up, this two-tenths heats up the flow after the flow moves smoothly through eight-tenths of the connection. There is a lot of flow now on the Earth but it's not making a complete contact, it gets caught and held and thus irritated within the atmosphere of your planet. Now, this is not meant to be a "scientific" discussion from a traditional sense, it is meant to be a discussion on the spiritual significance of the divine blueprinting system which we are calling dimensions and how to understand and use them to create a clearer individual life and a clearer joint life on the Earth.

We go on now to another **EXERCISE:** I'd like you to see your four body system standing side by side. On the left is your physical body, next to it on the right, your emotional and then the mental and then the spiritual. Now decide what color symbolically each of these bodies are to you right now. You might draw this out on a piece of paper and its really rather like a cut-out, meaning they're all cut from the same piece of paper, all attached together. The structures are attached so that you can't really separate one from the other but the colors are a focus of that particular body's expression.

Now the four bodies begin to move forward on a path and let's have that path golden, and you know that this is the purposeful path of your soul, the soul's purpose flowing now on the Earth - so you recognize that the golden path is within physical existence. You're coming to a city and the city represents, first of all, an area where all physical dimensions are, it also represents a focus of your soul's purpose as you recognize it now. Now there are four doors and each of your body's can choose to go into one of the doors. Now you will remember that I said that the four bodies are attached rather like a cut-out so how does that work? Well, because they cannot be separated, truly, when each body enters a door it will take one-fourth of every other body with it which is interesting if you think about it. Now you might number the four doors, again from the left, number one, number two, number three and number four. And ask your physical body which door it is going to go through Again you might assign a particular color to each door, not necessarily the same colors as the four body system. Ask your knowingness what color each door is.

Now, do this part of the exercise first. Move your four bodies towards the doors, seeing the doors and what colors they are, and then asking the bodies to make a choice and seeing them move through the door of their choice. Now, it probably won't be just really nice and neat with the physical body choosing door one, and the emotional door two etc. Three bodies may enter door number one or no bodies may enter door number one. Just do the exercise, take the four bodies into the city through whatever door they tell you they are going to enter.

Now, the next step will work as well as you allow it to do so. Don't finish this exercise right now. As soon as you've done the previous part of it try to forget it and then in perhaps a day or two or in even a week or two - you might put it on your calendar to look it up the next week. Don't go over what you've done but say to yourself,"now, which dimension was door number one? And which dimension was door number two? And which dimension was door number three? And which dimension was door number four?" Do this without trying to remember which doors your bodies went through - in other words, in order to be as objective or clear as possible ask your knowingness - was door number one the 3rd, 4th, 5th or the 6th dimension and write that down without refering which doors your bodies choose.

After you have completed that process then go back and see which bodies entered which dimension previously. It is important to recognize that as you grow in awareness of how to use the dimensions the way you use them will change and you may want to do this exercise several times remembering if you "cheat" by trying to manipulate your bodies going to a certain door, you simply defeat the purpose of the exercise and what you can gain from it.

It is important to be honest and objective and then from such honesty to build a bridge into a greater understanding of how to use the dimensions. Dimensional work is excellent for groups and if you are currently within a small group and studying together why don't you study this book together? Do the exercises together so that you can help each other to understand how you've used your four body system multi-dimensionally.

EXERCISE: View a river of electrical energy, a stream which moves and flows. You are within a small boat upon this river and you know that you've been flowing on it for quite some time. How does your emotional body feel about that stream of electrical energy? Is it enjoying it? Or is there some fear? Get in touch with your emotional body. Now, try to view the environment - what sort of an environment are you passing? Or are you passing? Is there a good flow, a good movement as you and your boat focus on this stream of electrical energy? I would do this exercise for two or three minutes only and then try to evaluate what you received.

Now if it flowed for you very well, and for many of you it will, then occasionally enjoy the boat exercise and the flow. It can be part of your 4th dimensional visualization which allows the Earth to move more easily into its

New Age potential. If you have difficulty seeing the boat move or if there is a lot of fear from this exercise then you have a block - either in regard to the electrical content or allowing your emotional body to be within the 4th dimension. Explore electrical areas - perhaps you've had a past life where you were struck by lightning or something else occurred where electricity seemed very dangerous. The 4th dimension focuses on a clearer usage of electrical magnetic energy within it and so the exploration of electrical magnetic energy and your relationship to it is important.

As you flow on your electrical river be sure you note the environment, that's why it's important to do this one for a while, even if it's easy and simply fun for you, note the environment because you can bring up, literally, from the subconscious certain areas for integration into your understanding as you view them on the flow.

An example might be: You suddenly pass a village that is almost destroyed, you know the bricks are very old and perhaps there's a castle there but most of it has been destroyed and no one lives there and yet you feel, "I know that village," it may be a past structure or pattern which you are still holding. No one lives there anymore, but the remnants are part of that two-tenths of resistance that yet exists in regard to completing the use of a 4th dimensional flowing structure.

In our example it didn't obscure the flow but perhaps if that old remnant, that old village was not there, that particular area could have been utilized in a clearer manner. It becomes then, a resistive point, so whatever you notice in your environment it is important to understand the meaning of it. You interpret it rather like you would a dream, symbolically knowing that it is talking about you. Now, it could be talking about the Earth too, on both levels, and you might get some interesting data about the Earth also doing this exercise.

EXERCISE: You see again your four bodies on a golden path and suddenly the path breaks up into many, many paths, almost without number, there are so many possibilities. Now your four bodies in this exercise need to agree upon one path - remember they are tied together. You might visualize this as rather like a sun's rays - all around a circle - and the four bodies now choose which focus within that whole circle they will energize.

Draw a circle with many, many lines all around it and ask your physical body which path it wants to explore. Put an "X" there. Then ask your emotional body which path it wants to explore and put an "X" there. Then ask your mental body which path it wants to explore and put an "X" there. Then ask your spiritual body which path it wants to explore and put an "X" there. It's not, my friends, that your bodies will always make the same choice, but at the present point of the "cosmic dance" you are doing they have made a choice thus ask them which choice they have made.

Next have a talk with your spiritual body and ask it to divide that circle up into four representing the four dimensions. Before you ask which is which simply divide from your center your circle into four sectors. Now I've given you an example to show you how it might look. Then through your communication with your spiritual body ask it to identify which part of the circle is which dimension. Again, I have given you an example and this is an example only, my friends. Then take a look at and see which bodies are functioning in which dimensions. In our example we see the following: the emotional body is functioning on the 3rd dimension, the mental body on the 5th dimension and the physical and spiritual bodies on the 4th dimension. This is not too bad a line up, actually. But it does contain some interesting emotionally stuck points, remembering that the 3rd dimension is magnification and creates some crystallization and resistances.

Our example person is having some emotional difficulties which are difficult to release, however, the mental perspective is in its natural house or home and able to analyze well and the physical structure and spiritual are flowing well together. Our example person probably enjoys the Earth and may meditate by running or walking or jogging and is bringing concepts into a flowing understanding well facilitated by the mental perspective in the 4th dimension, however, this is an example of someone which may very definitely bury their emotions because they are stuck and caught and difficult to deal with.

The fact that there is no contact yet, or at least at this point where we have focused the dimensional dance, there is no contact with the 6th dimension says that the overall blueprinting system hasn't yet been contacted particularly by the emotional body. This is not a far-out distribution of body's flowing dimensionally. I have used a rather common example. Many are moving into such an alignment by allowing the physical to enter the 4th dimension. The key, of course, is now allowing the emotional to enter the 4th dimension which will set up a flow to contact with the 6th dimension. Now as we look at this example we must realize that we have caught it at a particular beat, at a particular focus, at a particular part of the dimensional flow. It's like having a still-life photograph, I've said this before, the way they make early movies, and in order to see the full movement, you need many still-life photos and then they are put together but doing this over a period of time, perhaps until you have a hundred examples, taken over several months, will then give you a view of how you are using your four bodies multi-dimensionally.

Again, honesty is needed and being able to be objective in doing such an exercise, putting aside the desire to be progressing beyond your capabilities at this point, but because this is a exercise which is difficult to "fix", because you don't know really what is "best" it is rather easy to be honest with yourself. Remember, although at the beginning I told you that each body had a certain affinity for a specific dimension, the goal is <u>NOT</u>, I repeat, <u>IS NOT</u> to have that body function only in one dimension. Each dimension is there and life is only complete when each is utilized to create a whole. If you left out a part of this circle there would not be a completeness, you would have lost some strengths which that part of the circle or the dimension has brought to you.

I would try to see your dimensional focus, the one that you've just done with me, as looking at your life practically and as it is now, in the nowness. Now the nowness is always changing - change is the only constant that exists so it is necessary to recognize that there is an ideal.

That blueprinting system is the ideal and the way that you use it is affected by the ideal strengths that are inherently given to you by the Source itself. Thus, rather as an astrological chart talks about each planet having its home in one of the houses, the natural affinity that the 3rd dimension has for the physical body, the 4th dimension has for the emotional body, the 5th dimension for the mental body and the 6th dimension for the spiritual body tone the usage of the bodies awareness which is currently functioning in that dimension.

Now if you've been following me progressively in these exercises and I asked that you do that, then you will remember that in a previous exercise I told you that when one body chose to go through the door to the city it would take a portion of the other bodies with it. And it is necessary to really understand that - there is no possibility of completely isolating a body or a perspective - it's always going to be colored or affected in varying degrees by the other bodies or perspective. Even if you've buried your emotions they have been affected by their relationship with the other bodies, certainly with the spiritual perspective and certainly with the mental perspective and certainly now in physical existence with the physical perspective. Thus they have changed, they have grown, they have become more integrated - they are not what they were, they have evolved through their association with the other perspectives. Therefore, looking again at our previous sample person's usage of the four body system, you will note that in the 3rd dimension, the emotional body is focused there, that there is a perspective of the physical, spiritual, and mental present only through the emotional experience. So what we are really seeking to do through these exercises is to allow clarity of communication within the four body system. That's it. Clarity of communication so that whatever creative choices you make, as you dance multi-dimensionally the four body system can communicate with each other and flow your potential through the communicative link which is then allowed.

The most important thing that you can do in learning to use the dimensions clearly is to keep the four bodies communicating with one another. Thus, in the final portion of this exercise, use the outcome of your own exercise and have each of the bodies communicate and tell the other bodies what its like where they are. Going back to our example: the emotional body which is centered in your 3rd dimension can explain to the mental perspective how it is to be in the 3rd dimension. Now the mental body in the 5th dimension doesn't relate too well to the emotional body in the 3rd dimension. There is, usually a resistive pattern where the mental body will say, "oh, my goodness - look at those emotions - they're stuck and caught again," good communication is necessary to progress the understanding of how to use that format. It's not so much moving the bodies around arbitrarily within the dimensions but allowing wherever they are to be more clearly understood and thus allowingness, tolerance, love and trust is established within the four body system.

Certainly, there are some clearer usages than others but you will need to understand where you are now and through such understanding allow the process to become that love centered, love focused life you are seeking. Most of you need to be more loving and allowing of yourself as well as others, of your own efforts, of your own use of the dimensions as that is our subject.

I would suggest, then, that you personify your bodies, or have a friend work with you and take the role of your body where you bring forth the point of view that you're trying to understand and the friend brings forth the other bodies that are trying to understand it. In other words, in our example of the emotional/mental on the 3rd and the 5th dimension, you could be the emotional perspective and explain to your friend who represents your mental 5th dimensional focus perspective what's going on. The mental will reply - there will be a communicative link established and thus a clearer understanding can come about as to how you have used that 3rd dimensional focus.

Do you see that change and evolution simply means using the system more clearly. We always have the system given to us by the Source in our active state of beingness, in our functioning within the plan, within the cosmic plan. What changes is not the system but how we use it, how we see it, how we open to it, how we trust it, how we integrate it, how we respond to the openings that are created within it. Thus communication within a particular usage of the four body system multi-dimensionally will show you a way to use the system in a clearer manner.

EXERCISE: See yourself traveling down a highway in a vehicle. Note first what sort of vehicle you have selected. Is it a car? A train? A motorcycle? Please keep it on the physical level. Note its condition, note its color and then as you now travel you reach the first area that you're going to visit so your highway has a turn off here. You take the exit. And you go into a specific area. Note the environment, is it a large metropolitan area? Is it a small village, is it the seashore? The mountains? Note the environment. First then, write down on a sheet of paper what vehicle you have selected and the condition of your vehicle, then note the first stop, a little bit about it - briefly and literally how many days you would like to visit it. Spend five minutes in doing this. When it is completed you get in your vehicle and you get back on your highway and you go to the second stop.

You turn off here - note the distance between the first and second stop in miles - what does your speedometer tell you - how many miles have you gone since the first stop? Repeat the process as you did in Number One, spending about five minutes on developing it. When you have completed your visit, get back on your highway, noting the distance between the second and third stops. Turn off at the exit way. In the third stop, you are looking for a road, a different road which will take you back home, back where you began.

You know that there is one, see how that develops. You may have to ask someone. Note what process you go through to find it, but after finding it then get on it and travel home and note what kind of a road it is - a mountain road, a winding road, a straight six lane highway, a small road that wanders through village after village, a limited access road but not a freeway. See what road you select. When you have returned home then you have completed your dimensional journey. Each stop represents a dimension. The 3rd, the 4th and the 5th. Seek to see the characteristics of each stop and see if you can figure out which is which. Now because of your willingness to do this exercise I have assisted you so that you haven't just visited the 3rd dimension, you have, actually had an experience in each of the three - the 3rd, 4th and 5th.

The final part of this exercise is to see in your home that a stairway exists that you hadn't noticed before - you may ask: "when did they build that stairway and where does it go?" And the answer will come back: "while you were on your trip." Why don't you go up and see where it goes? I'd like you to climb that stairway and note its condition, its size, its shape - what type of a stairway it is. Note how long the stairway is. Now you reach a door that opens and as you go into this new area you will note that you have a broad overview of the whole highway which you traveled and all three stops that you made. You will see all of this now from the point of view of the 6th dimension which can view and interact with and be a part of all of the other physical dimensions. Now the 6th dimension and your viewing from it can help you clarify or understand the other three adventures which you have had. So if there is something you didn't completely understand about one of your visits then while, in your higher 6th dimensional focus ask about it and actually see this higher dimension or expression clarifying for you the true meaning of each experience.

Earlier in this book I gave you a little different way to look at the dimensions. This exercise shows you the clearest and most precise way of contacting the 6th dimension. It permeates the others and creates a unified dimensional structure because it represents the divine blueprint area. I refer you to the earlier material for further understanding of the 6th dimension.

EXERCISE: I'd like you to see a circle, there is a point where you are standing within that circle. You are facing one way, a counter-clockwise direction, behind you is a focus we will call the 3rd dimension. In front of you is a focus called the 4th dimension, put an "X" there where you are standing and label these dimensions, the 3rd behind and the 4th in front as you go counter-clockwise around the circle, then there is a bridge and a focus called the 5th dimension. With your knowingness choose two points farther around the circle to delineate the beginning and end of the 5th dimension and label the dimension. The whole circle itself is the 6th dimension. This is a more complete way of understanding dimensions. Earlier in this book I gave you a little different way to look at the dimensions. There is an illustration on the next page,

DIAGRAM #1

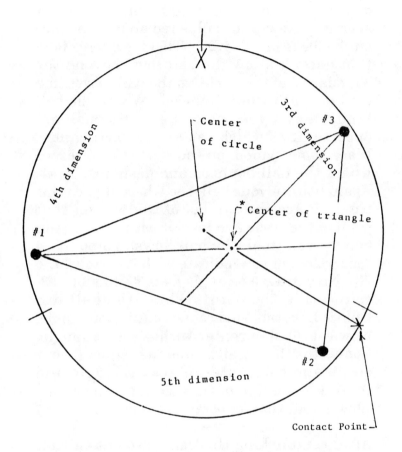

Contact Point comes out to be in the 5th Dimension
which indicates that in this person's case the 5th
dimension (structures) is the main focus and more
should be studied with regard to this dimension.

    * Center of triangle is found by connect-
      ing the midpoints of two of the sides to
      their respective opposite angles. Where
      these lines cross is the center of the
      triangle

Diagram #1, showing how to set this up.

The "X" in the illustration shows you the focus of your awareness at the beginning of our exercise. Now your ball is red and you bounce on the focus marked "X". There is a force field that doesn't allow the ball to go beyond the boundaries of the circle, so the ball moves in a circular path when bounced. Where the ball lands shows you the focus of dimensional opportunities which you are contacting now. Place some symbol on the circle to represent where the ball bounced and designate it #1. Again bounce your ball, see where it goes this time. Place the symbol of the ball on that point of the circle and label it with a #2. Again bounce your ball, the ball flows to a point on the circle and you indicate with its symbol the #3. Now draw a triangle from #1 to #2 to #3, connecting the points where the ball has bounced. Establish a center within your circle. Now establish a center within your triangle. Connect with a straight line the center of your circle and the center of your triangle and continue this line until it contacts the circle. This is your contact point on the circle.

After establishing this contact point on your circle, note the dimension that it falls in. This point is important in your present understanding. It indicates the dimension which is a strength and can be used to assist you in a more multi-dimensional connection. Draw a straight line from the focus of where you bounced your ball - the gateway of the 4th dimension - to this important focus which you have perceived through the previous exercise. Study the dimensional material given about that dimension, see its strengths, how can you use it to help you understand your life more clearly? You are currently bouncing your life from that point of view, expressing from it, if you will.

This volume is not a volume to just read once, it is literally a textbook on dimensional understanding, absorb as much as you can, learn to really understand what the dimensions mean so that each exercise will speak to you clearly of the strengths which you are using in your life. It will, of course, also point out the needed areas where life is not flowing as completely as you would like.

EXERCISE: View a grid system, vertical and horizontal lines criss-crossing. Now you may wish to draw it on a piece of paper. I would suggest that it be at least six inches square with at least six lines intersecting both directions. Again, you have a bouncing ball. Now, above your grid system, which represents the dimensions, is a satellite and we will call it the spiritual residence of your soul. This is for exercise purposes only as it is rather a distortion of a soul relationship.

See yourself on this satellite as your soul and you have your ball. You're going to bounce it into the grid system. You, as the soul, view the grid system. Looking down at it you recognize that the satellite itself in which you reside sends an electrical impulse which has created the grid system. So you as a soul know its your grid system but you also know that the level of the soul which will use the grid system makes choices in how to use it. Literally the ball represents the projection of the soul into the grid system and the ball has its own level of consciousness also.

You as the soul then bounce the ball into the grid system. It then becomes conscious of its own movement and its own life. It has been created through the soul's projection of the divine blueprinting system into physical existence. Alright, in our exercise then, see yourself as the soul bouncing the ball into the grid system. Put an "X" where it contacts the grid system and also a "1". Now you will note that the ball continues to bounce, in fact the bouncing is eternal. We can slow it down, which is what physical existence does to the projection of consciousness as it is initiated by each divine level of consciousness.

Let's follow it through twelve steps. First: Put an "X1" where it bounces the first time and where it bounces next put an "X2". Let the ball continue to bounce 12 times and mark each spot it bounces into, each square, with a number as you did for the first two bounces.

Now in a contrasting color I suggest that you connect the points going from One, to two, to three, to four, to five, to six, to seven, to eight, to nine, to ten, to eleven and to twelve. Then from twelve go back to number one. We will call that an incarnation. We will say that each number represents five years sequentially and thus after having completed the twelfth five-year focus that personality or projection is pulled back into the soul or what humanity calls death on the physical level. This does not mean that you will spend five years in each one of these squares but the synchronicity of the numbers for a particular time period shows you that you have a connective flow moving from one point dimensionally to the next and progressing it in a overall sense in relationship to the 6th dimension. Please understand that the previous exercise is in relationship to the 6th dimension and only that.

The grid system represents the 6th dimension and its relationship with all of the other dimensions. Interestingly enough if you passed over one square or one area more than once in your grid system, let us say number one and number six were in the same square in your grid system they may be energized as completely different dimensions, number one may be the 3rd dimension while number six may be the 5th although they may seem to be in the same "space" within the 6th dimensional grid system.

This means that when we reach the 6th dimension and seek to understand it, although it may interact with time and space you can't view the grid system and understand it in relationship to a 3rd dimensional grid system which will have a definite "territory" for each of the dimensions. The 6th dimension seeks to instruct us in continuity of consciousness and constructing the ideal which has been projected into physicality using an energy flow which is so united that its projection focus simply moves multi-dimensionally as needed to respond to the consciousness direction given to it by the "ball" or soul thrust which occupies that grid work system.

Certainly, understanding the 6th dimension will take a little "time" but get a glimpse of it now through seeing the overlap of the dimensions within the 6th dimensional grid system and that there really isn't any one space for each dimension but a communicative linkage system which is what the dimensions represent.

EXERCISE: Before you is a rainbow and you are standing and looking at it. You can see each color blending into the next color. As you view the rainbow it becomes a circle so that every color slides into every other color and the circle turns into a spiral. Stand in the center of that circle and allow the spiral of colors to move up through you. It is spiraling up and you are standing on the base of that circle of rainbow colors as it becomes a spiral. The colors flow all around you and because they are moving, spiraling, they are constantly changing. You are coming in contact with blue here and orange there. Violet and indigo, yellow and green and red. The positioning of the colors is constantly changing because of the movement of the spiral. The spiral moves, turns, and your association with a particular color moves to a different perspective. Spend five or ten minutes sitting in this ever changing rainbow, this kaleidoscope of color movement.

This literally is one way of viewing the dimensions. There are changing levels of awareness which blend and flow creating an awareness kaleidoscope that is ever sensitive to changing directives from a Source perspective whether you consider that Source to be the overall plan or you as you evolve and grow. The change is the blueprinting or grid system projected by your soul flowing ever more completely. One has only to accept the change to participate within it in a progressively more conscious manner.

Dimensions assist the focusing of consciousness so that the understanding or expanding of consciousness is ever assisted by this overall kaleidoscope or by the Source's interaction with the self. You can look at the overall Source level or at the kaleidoscope of colors as symbolic. The colors represent your will, your heart, your emotional, mental and physical perspectives, your mind, your receptive and dynamic energies, your physical senses and much more. The small pieces of colored plastic in the kaleidoscope represent the above aspects of self and as they interact with each other they are constrained by their shapes and the shape of the container into specific type of interaction, just as the dimensions both limit and support consciousness.

If you are creating a dessert and you simply put in a little chocolate, a little vanilla, a little orange, a little lemon, a little peppermint, a little of this and a little of that and you blend it up you may get a dessert but you may be surprised how it tastes. A rainbow is a blending of colors or flavors which allows easy identification but strengthens each color through its association with the others. The rainbow utilizes a dimensional type structure for definition and support.

While sitting in your spiral of dimensional strengths you may notice certain colors passing by: for example, your right eye - there is a flash of red, there is green, there is blue and yellow and violet, orange is present also. Each color is literally a perspective of life which is unique, but which is connected with every other life perspective.

EXERCISE: See or know that you are walking on a beautiful field of blue. As you begin to walk on it, it seems alive and you recognize that it is growing. There is under your feet a sense of life itself. You recognize that there is growth there. Now move along on it and you will come to a particular point on this blue field where there is a magic button which you can press if you are willing. Press it, and you will note an elevator door appears, opens and you can get on the elevator. Do so.

Now the doors will close behind you and again you will have a sense of movement. It really isn't different than the previous movement except we've added the doors so that you can see a change as it comes about.

Ride along in your elevator and you may not have a sense that you are going up or down, just movement is appropriate. If you feel you are going up and down, that's alright, that's fine but what you want to feel is the sense of movement, of flow, as if you were riding on an ocean or a large lake in a very large ship which has good stabilizers. Ride for a while until the doors open and you are then going to get out, going to go through the door into a particular scene which you have created through your sense of movement or change. Now because of the nature of these exercises, the angelic kingdom is assisting with this change and will assist in bringing you a scene to clarify your understanding of movement or change. The ability to allow movement or change is what is called the flow or the use of the 4th dimension. So as you go through your doors you will see a scene which is helpful to you in allowing change. You may get a glimpse of a past experience when change was difficult, you may get a glimpse of an opportunity which may be coming to you and will change your life if you allow it. Whatever it is, go through your door and see what, through the assistance of the angelic kingdom, you can learn about the flow or change.

In my opinion this exercise, although simple, is for many of you the key to understanding how to create both the type of life you want for yourself and that type of New Age peaceful, harmonious expression you all want for the Earth. Now, if you get into a scenario which you do not understand, you can erase it or go into your elevator again. Ride until the elevator doors open and while you are in there ask for another scenario which will help you or will clarify for you the first experience. Many of you know that if you have a dream and you can't figure out what it means you can ask for another dream to interpret the first one. Thus, if you get into a scenario which you do not understand or cannot interpret then ask for another scenario to explain the first one to you. Perhaps in a variation of this exercise you can see the clearest use of the dimensions.

This is a variation of the above exercise. You step onto the blue and you sense the movement. You come to a large building where there are three elevators and you may choose which button to push to call one of the elevators. You call that elevator and you step into it. The doors shut and you allow the movement of the elevator until the doors open. You view that experience, learn from it, you then go back to the bank of the elevators and push a second elevator button. You get on that elevator from your association with the scenario brought to you from the first elevator. Thus you progress by going into the second elevator asking that this experience be elevated to a clearer level.

Now the difference between the first exercise and this one is that in the first exercise if you do not understand a scenario you ask and are given another experience to explain it. In this second variation, where you have a building and you're going up in the elevator, you really progress from a perspective that is the personality level to the second perspective which of the soul level and if you wish you can push the third elevator button, after the second scenario and ask to be connected through that elevator to the monadic level. Your three scenarios will be joined through all of the dimensions.

The dimensions are the means to go from one to the other, to move your consciousness from one focus to another, they literally create the focuses so that evolution "holds still" for you enough that you can learn and expand from viewing it That is quite important. If you didn't get off the elevator occasionally, look around and see what is being projected dimensionally existence would be a gentle blur and you really would not be able to identify one another or any opportunities which presented themselves. When you are born into a physical body the first few months are needed to adjust to the use of multi-dimensions, to the flow of dimensions, to the interaction of dimensions and to the focus on dimensions.

A baby's focusing ability is not yet dimensionalized when they are born. They do not really see beyond the gentle blurring of all colors, and sounds. Now this is changing, many babies are beginning to identify dimensional structure at an earlier age, some as young as three months.

Before that there is still a gentle rainbow which moves, which talks many times, because with the child it is generally the mother and father and others in the environment who represent the rainbow to the child. Gradually the child learns to get off the elevator enough so that a focus is created and ability to differentiate the mother, for example, the parts of its physical body and the physical environment itself. You may think about the child coming into awareness of the 3rd dimension - and that is true, but a clearer way of viewing it is to see that the child is really learning to use the changes of moving inter-dimensionally in a focused and yet free-flowing manner. He is learning from its birth to use a new opportunity to look at life through an electrical grid system, a flow pattern, a kaleidoscope of colors, a rainbow - all of the above are various ways of addressing or talking about dimensions.

Physical existence does not shut out the use of the higher dimensions. It's just that when you push the button on that elevator and move into those higher dimensions you do so in the sleep state. You haven't yet learned how to bring your physical body into that dimensional flow. Eventually you will, if you wish, learn how to do that. I, Vywamus, can have a physical structure in my use of all dimensions,

I don't but I could. The reason I don't is that it serves no particular purpose to have it here but if in a future cosmic expression it would serve a purpose then I certainly could create it.

As you learn to understand dimensions you will begin to see that the flowing of consciousness has chosen what we call dimensions as a means to maintain a contact with what it has realized in various experiences. The dimensions then become literally a storage system for knowledge, for understanding and certainly for expressing the qualities of Sourceness.

CHAPTER 3

MULTI-DIMENSIONAL OPERATION

The dimensions are used in connection with one another but in any sort of divine activity there is usually a base or premise that is focused through one dimension. An example would be music. Music and its flow are focused through the 4th dimension, but depending upon the vibrational level, the music may flow from the 4th to the 3rd, touch into the 5th , circle into the 6th and then perhaps come back to the 4th. This is but an example. One reason your national anthem, The Star Spangled Banner, is so thrilling and so effective is its unique use of the 6th dimension. Although it has a 4th dimensional focus, its slide multi-dimensionally unites the perspective of everyone who hears it. All great national anthems have this quality and humanity instinctively picks such an inspirational piece of music for their national anthem.

Some music moves multi-dimensionally in a smooth, rhythmic manner, other music darts or moves in a almost dis-jointed manner multi-dimensionally. Such music in its sudden changes, in its rhythmic surprises, is composed by the modern musical geniuses whose rhythms move from the ordinary to the unexpected within a measure or two. There may be a rapid movement from one easily defined rhythm into a counterpoint rhythm which is a dimensional switch or change. Many times the dimension will only be explored for three or four bars before either moving back or on to a yet different rhythmic or dimensional experience. Each particular rhythm in music expresses a dimension but not always the same one. It isn't that simple to define dimensions.

Rhythmically the quality of life is projected by the composer into a pattern of sound which dips and soars dimensionally. Each dimensional excursion will be unique within the expression, not only of the composer, but of the one that performs that piece of music. Many of you have heard a song sung in one manner and then another singer will perform it in an entirely different manner. This is a different dimensional use. Many times it is the emotional body (it represents the flow you know) that expresses or moves emotionally within a piece of music.

Perhaps the most, to me anyway, interesting and complete music created on this planet is created by composers who are able to move inter-dimensionally in their creativeness with all of their bodies. In other words, their music expresses the Earth, it expresses the soul, it expresses divine structure, it expresses the divine flow in an intricate and ever expanding manner. It is absolutely thrilling to listen to the movement or through the sound to sense the dimensions mingling and expanding. A concert then literally represents a dimensional exercise, everyone that participates in the concert is taken along or flows dimensionally with everyone else. Perhaps not precisely the same but there is enough compatibility in the flow that the concert creates a powerful vortex or energy. The angelic kingdom enjoys concerts because it can harvest a great deal of energy for use in the plan from them.

Sports are dimensional experiences. Each sport presents a dimensional experience in a little different manner. Football is uniting the 3rd and 4th dimensions but the 5th dimension is used in a manner which seeks to allow a new level of contact which is called the goal. Two teams or two focuses are both trying to project to the goal. Each is seen as an opposition to one another. However, no matter who wins the game, everyone who participates and everyone who watches makes contact with that new level called the goal. It's interesting to see the projection of winning and losing put into a dimensional framework. Those who "win", when they reach their goal, allow a contact with this goal which gives them a feeling of freedom, self confidence and accomplishment. Those who "lose" although they too have reached the goal, finished the game, don't identify with the goal as being theirs. It seems to be someone else's goal and the lack of identification with it sometimes causes a sense of frustration and difficulty in accepting the goal as theirs.

The "winning" mode in sports or in life is simply an identification process which makes real for you the use of the dimensional contacts you have made to the point of realization which allows them to flow in a unification of the four-body system which is, my friends, the plan.

The divine plan is literally a consciousness exercise which creatively explores and learns from a particular overall theme. Reaching a point of connection with a goal and identifying that as a "win" can only be done when the use of the dimensions is clear enough that your emotions, your mental perspective and your physical perspective are united into a spiritual perspective which recognizes you as part of the overall team. The key to the use of the dimensions is feeling a part of the process, is accepting that your perspective is one that is valid, appreciated, supported and therefore can expand. Without creative self confidence there is a "no-win" situation. Your team seems to have lost and it plunges many of you into the emotional pits or into an over and over need to analyze from every point of view why you didn't "win". Some bury their emotions then overuse the mental structure in seeking to understand the "no-win" situation, going over and over the past activity to learn from it. It is not necessary to either be in an emotional pit or a circle of mental hyperactivity which is compulsive. You can play the game by recognizing the dimensional structure is there as a support system for everyone and you can meet and connect with others by means of it.

What you may not recognize is that without the dimensions you'd never know about one another because you would not be able to focus the kaleidoscope or rainbow enough to differentiate its parts or to see other people. All you would sense would be blurs or color, of movement, and every time you tried to communicate with one another your hearing wouldn't cooperate with your speaking and your touching couldn't make contact with another either. The dimensions are the tools then which allow consciousness or each of you to contact each other. The Source talks to tself through the dimensions. You are all its various parts.

On the 9th dimension there is an experimental laboratory which prototypes new cosmic days. Earlier in this material I talked about Cosmic Days which had been pulled back because they didn't work and they are now completing in the 8th dimension. A prototyping of possible Cosmic Days also is necessary and literally every one of you has partaken in these prototyping experiences. Some of you have gained your strengths, have opened doors for yourself through these prototyping experiences. Some of you have learned about other color possibilities, other sound possibilities, other means of expressing that expanded your awareness much beyond what it had been. I'd like to give you one example here because it is quite a wide spread example that many of you have experienced in this prototyping area.

A prototyping experience usually begins at the time of the birth of a new Cosmic Day. Those of you that are going to be active on that Cosmic Day receive your training and you begin the days activities. Everyone else is supporting the Cosmic Day in one way or another. A certain percentage of divine beings, however, are involved in research and we could call it the use of consciousness. Beyond just a few well educated scientists there will be those that have little experience, those that have a great deal of experience, those that are specialists in many areas, those that are generalists in many areas, in other words, the research will utilize every point of view to be complete.

One prototype is the divine garden. Because of its infinite variety it has been used a great deal. You enter the laboratory of the prototyping experience and you are "dipped" into a particular type of expression. It would be like receiving a certain type of physical structure, perhaps shaped like a balloon or perhaps a structure that has twelve arms, perhaps a structure that is like a two-headed physical being with four arms and legs. It isn't always physical but it sometimes is. Use your imagination and see that you have probably been in one of these prototypes within some exotic structure. You may be able to go back and remember that. It may be very helpful to do so because it will open to you what you learned in that expression, helping to free you from the perception that only your current structure is comfortable because it is familiar. It is not that you will probably ever use that structure again, whatever exotic type it might have been, but it frees you to expand into the understanding that structure moves, flows, changes, evolves and each unique structural expression has opened you in a manner which progresses your understanding.

Now in the divine garden experience you were usually given a role to play. Let us say, just for example, that you were shaped like a balloon and in your expression you were given a corridor to bounce in. You bounced again the walls and the ceilings, we will put this in the 3rd dimension, although it may not have been, but you could bounce anywhere you wanted.

You see at the other end of the corridor another balloon. Let us say that you are blue in color and you note that this other balloon is slightly larger and its a yellow and orange stripe. You note its beauty and you feel attracted to it but it is at the other end of the corridor. Now you decide to move to it but you find you don't know how to do that. As you try to propel yourself forward in the corridor you bounce off the ceiling and then you bounce off the side of the walls and then you bounce off the floor and pretty soon you're back where you started - frustrated - not sure how to move. Gradually, through trial and error you note how to move. You may think you have the hang of it - you have discovered movement and then suddenly you're back where you started again.

At this point you decide to project your consciousness to the balloon at the other end of the corridor. Surprisingly this works very well and there is an instant recognition by that consciousness of you. You try to talk to the other balloon but again you find you don't know how. You try to make a sound and what you get is something that doesn't mean anything or at least you can't understand it. However, the other balloon is also seeking to communicate and gradually, although you are yet apart physically, you're structures haven't yet learned to negotiate space, your consciousness is learning to communicate. In the meantime you're also working on physical movement so now the conscious movement through communication is going on, and you're also learning to move physically.

Eventually you negotiate the corridor, coming into contact with the other balloon. Let us say you enjoy being together, you in your blueness snuggle up to the orange-yellow larger balloon and after a period of time you look around and what you see are small balloons, all around you, some of them are blue, some of them are yellow, some of them are orange. There is an expansion from your contact with the other balloon. In this simple example we note that the new-born consciousness must recognize it can communicate in many ways and these various ways are through different levels of consciousness which are called physical, mental, emotional and spiritual. But in order to keep them straight, in order to allow a definition of these levels, dimensions support the effort and one must learn to negotiate or move within each dimension, to utilize it as a communicative tool.

Thus the balloon had to learn to move in the corridor and also to "speak" in consciousness within that corridor to the other balloon. The corridor itself represents the 3rd and also the 4th dimension as movement occurs. The 5th dimension is the shape of the corridor, the overall dimension, the structure of it. The 6th dimension is the lifting of consciousness by the balloon which then projected to the other balloon. The lifting effect is an important key to the use of any multi-dimensional structure because it contacts the 6th dimension. You will note in our example that through the lifting of the consciousness the two balloons found their compatibility factor. They found they liked each other. Although they could not yet approach each other physically, the uniting of the consciousness within the 6th dimension allowed a magnetic attraction that drew them together physically.

The clearest way to attract a relationship partner is by going to the spiritual level where the divine blueprint "lives", going within that divine blueprint until your knowingness contacts another being, another consciousness, finding the compatibility factor there, allowing that relationship to grow until it becomes so magnetic at that level that it expands into a multi-dimensional expression. Many of you think it is necessary to find a relationship partner physically first but in the relationships which last the longest or at least are the most effective, it truly is a spiritual unity which creates a magnetic attraction which literally draws together the other bodies, the mental, emotional, and usually, at last, the physical.

Those relationships which start with the physical, the sexual urges, the physical attraction, don't necessarily fail but many of them do because the relationship hasn't learned to negotiate the multi-dimensional expression which is the only truly satisfying and full way to have a relationship. Without uniting on every level there is never a long lasting compatibility in a relationship. It satisfies on one level for a while but unless that level expands into another level or unless the unity has already been established on other levels the partners will probably wander from each other looking for a more complete relationship.

Completeness within a relationship is what is sought because when it is there, there is a sense of support and yet a loving, expanding, creative journey together. Whether or not one has a physical relationship partner the journey of unity is sought on every level. You as a human being are seeking unity within humanity. You are seeking to recognize you are a part of the team of humanity, you are seeking to understand you are an equal partner within the ranks of humanity. Certainly at times you are a leader, at other times others are the leaders. You are seeking to see your connection with humanity. You may not be conscious of this yet but your commitment to the Earth, to service of the plan is in one respect a commitment to humanity. This too is a polarity joining - you and humanity. You have a very special relationship with humanity, we may take this a step further and say that you are part of groups in many ways - one of those groups is humanity.

Now in a mirroring process on the physical level you will learn from humanity because many creative experiences will be undergone by you, flowing them multi-dimensionally so that you can understand your own polarity relationship in connection with humanity. Now in this polarity relationship you play both roles at one time or another. Sometimes you receive from humanity or play the female. Sometimes you are the male or the thrust for humanity. One might say sometimes you are the student and sometimes you are the teacher. Your polarity relationship with humanity is physical in your interaction with other people, it's emotional in your feelings in regard to other people, it's mental in your sharing ideas with other people and it's spiritual in the ability to unite your purposes together to create a productive Earth environment. This too is a flow of dimensional structure, the development of your clearer understanding of your relationship with humanity.

Time and time again you will experience what you believe about that relationship until you have resolved the issues, clarified them to the point where you feel unified creatively with humanity. This is an extremely important area of understanding for each of you. Some of you may not know that you have some resistance in this area. All of you have some. Some have more than others. If you understood your relationship with humanity completely you would no longer be on the Earth. The Christ, your great world teacher and Avatar, is an excellent example of being clear in relationship to humanity. He knew humanity very well, he knew their weaknesses, the knew their strengths, he had great appreciation and understanding of humanity.

That was why he could tell his disciples what they would do and how they would act, he knew them well - he understood humanity. Probably he and the Lord Maitreya, the Christ, and Djwahl Khul understand humanity more than any other spiritual teacher who is connected with your Earth. Certainly Sanat Kamara, the planetary logos understands them quite well but the the Lord Maitreya has a special ability to see humanity's relationship with itself, to understand how it will create within a particular multi-dimensional flow which is called an experience. Experiences are then the use of the dimensions in a unique manner. Each experience uses dimensions in a little different manner.

Although a rock concert and a classical Beethoven symphony are both musical they use the dimensional structure completely differently. The Lord Maitreya, in my opinion, is your resident expert in dimensional understanding. The reason why humanity can sense who he is, can feel his love and appreciate the Lord Maitreya perhaps more than any other teacher, at least in this time period, is his unification of the dimensions which assist others in unification.

In the Christ's parables, his stories, his teaching, the goal was to show humanity a unified point of view, a perspective which allowed a progression of understanding beyond a point that seemed stuck within humanity. The prodigal son is a good example and this example shows at the time the Christ was on the Earth an area which needed a more unified understanding beyond a point which the Christ saw as a resistive use of multi-dimensional structure. Each of his stories, his parables, and you only have about five percent in your written literature of the ones he told left then assisted others in releasing resistance to multi-dimensional flow.

The Cabala is a great multi-dimensional tool. Each of the dimensions and the corridors are well represented. The dimensional focuses are divided into 9 plus the emergence or Source point but they aren't numbered in the same manner that I have numbered the dimensions. The reason that I mention the Cabala is that the Christ was a great Caballist and his wisdom used the understanding of Caballistic principles to help humanity by pinpointing blocks within the multiple grid system of Caballistic philosophy and flow. One correlation I wish to make here with the Cabala and what I have brought forth is this: the Cabala has three pillars, a right, a left and a center pillar. My point here is not to give you a course on Caballistic principles but to show you that from one point of view these three pillars represent being focused in the 3rd dimension, expressing through two polarities. If we created a tree of life, as the Cabala calls it, in another Cosmic Day we might have four or five pillars rather than three. The 3rd dimension represents the deepest plunge into expression which the Source currently expresses. Thus it becomes the basis or the framework within which to "hang" different dimensions which will then support the various levels of consciousness as they move, flow, dance and joyously create, also as they communicate because at the core of all of creation is literally the need to communicate, the need to explore, the Source's need to explore itself.

The 3rd dimension is not something we are releasing in the sense the Earth is getting off it but it is being seen, as the three pillars are in the Cabala, as a fundamental principle upon which the consciousness can build a complete house or structure. I am saying this several times in several ways so that you understand that you will always have within you the 3rd dimensions and what you've learned there. You are just learning to use the 3rd dimension more clearly as a basis for everything else but not to feel stuck, caught or limited by it.

In an interesting aside here your physical abilities of coordination and spontaneous reaction physically are multiplying at this time as the 4th dimension is recognized. Athletes will jump farther, run faster, each function which requires physical coordination will become easier for those who allow themselves to enter the flow accessing the 4th dimension.

CHAPTER 4

FATTY TISSUE (CELLULITE) A STUCK DIMENSIONAL PERSPECTIVE

For a while as this 4th dimension is recognized the recognition of it will allow a cleansing of the 3rd dimensional structure, old resistances, old patterns of behavior, old patterns of relationship with your physical body can be released. Let us say the shape of your physical body is not what you want. There may be deposits of fat in inappropriate areas or so you believe. Visualizing your physical body in a more flowing state daily, seeing it moving into the 4th dimension will begin to release some of those more stubborn cellulite deposits which have perhaps been something you wanted to get rid of.

Cellulite or what you call "fat" is simply a stuck dimensional perspective. The most resistive deposits are in the areas on your physical body which symbolically relate to a area that is not yet clearly understood. You are not clear in a particular area. Although the intention of this book is not to give every detail of the dimensions, such a work would be impossible, I do want to give you now certain keys to the cellulite area physically because they are stuck perspectives in that area of entering the 4th dimension.

95

Symbolically cellulite in the area of the upper thighs represents difficulty in unifying the perspective of the polarities. Difficulty is experienced in understanding the equality of the polarities, there is usually a swing back and forth between polarity usage. There is movement but it is difficult to unite it. Look deeply in the polarity area reconciling the swings and you will find that the cellulite in this upper thigh area will disappear.

The cellulite in the upper hips is a settling in to the 3rd dimension. Many times the personality seems stubbornly attached to one way of living. Change is difficult and it is seen as threatening to the comfort of life and to allowing the life to become a changing perspective. Change is very difficult and when the relationship with change is clearer the cellulite in this area will disappear.

In the upper arm area cellulite indicates an acceptance of a condition of limitation which is held onto because there is the need to be secure. Insecurity and unworthiness are the symbols. Look deeply into your connection with the Source itself, feeling worthy to express beyond what you are currently holding onto.

Cellulite in the seat area is a build-up of resistance, a layered effect, you literally sit on resistance and in one sense you keep piling it up, not releasing it until you can see it physically. It means that in at least three or four important areas you have a multi-leveled resistive effect which needs to be explored. The key for you if the cellulite is in the seat area is to accept responsibility for creating your life - that you truly have created it in a step-by-step manner and now you are not stuck or sitting eternally in all of the effects you have created but can, layer by layer, level by level release the build-up of what has accumulated. Acknowledging self responsibility and being willing to be patient and peel the onion of consciousness, peeling away levels gradually is a key to releasing cellulite in this area. Truly cultivating self responsibility and patience are keys in this area.

If you have cellulite around the middle, the waist, the back and the stomach area the cause, is in the area of being supported and nurtured. The Source level connection needs to be clear. It may be that many areas of your Source level relationship are quite clear already because in one sense you have recognized a strong relationship or you wouldn't have the need for it. If you didn't believe there was a Source at all you wouldn't be concerned about it. The clarifying of the divine support area and the need to be nurtured will release structural blockages which create cellulite in these areas.

The breasts are symbolic of a compulsive need to nurture others. It is so compulsive that levels of resistance have built up to the point where they heavily endow the physical structure. There is always a misunderstanding of the role, of the responsibility area. In point of fact, although nurturing is the most easily perceived symbol in the breast area, the true key to releasing the cellulite is clearing the area of responsibility. Literally the cellulite here is saying, "I build up more and more responsibility into the structure but it isn't flowing, it isn't moving through me, its accumulating within me, I haven't yet seen how to allow it to flow." There may be, not in all cases, but in at least 50% an accompanying area of abundance, not necessarily lack of abundance but non-clarity in how to place it in the responsibility area.

Cellulite on the upper back area represents difficulty in the electrical area. The soul is electrical in nature as you know and coming into the physical structure it is grasped literally by the endocrine or glandular system and the thyroid, parathyroid, adrenal, pituitary, pineal, thymus and gonad areas not given in any particular order here have through their secreting of hormones allowed for many of you a build-up of cellulite in direct correlation to the amount of clarity that you have in the electrical flow area. It almost always accumulates mainly in the upper back area, however, there may also be a build-up in the area of the knees, around the neck and sometimes the ankles. Electrical clarity needs to be worked on in many ways by all of you.

If there are cellulite deposits sprinkled all over throughout the physical body, many times flexibility is the area which is resistive and is the area which when understood more clearly and allowed more comprehensively will release the cellulite from the physical structure. Now the reason I use the cellulite in this book on dimensions is for some of you, at least, it is easier to see resistances if they are right there on your physical structure. It also "proves" my point if in reading this you develop an understanding of an area that allows the cellulite to disappear. A group of you who read this book and there will be many such groups might set up a program to see the correlations with the cellulite as I have given it and the resolutions from clearing the consciousness in these specific areas.

There are a few with cellulite deposits on the feet and this indicates a basic resistance area almost always Source level related, the resistance to being in physical existence, the resistance to being individualized, the resistance to being anywhere except within the arms or within the womb of Source. Beliefs that through the individualization process and through becoming physical there has been a loss or a "tossing out" of the consciousness. Such beings with this type of cellulite are always seeking to "go home" not yet recognizing that home is within their own understanding of the divine linkage system.

Cellulite then, an interesting symbol in the area of resistances, resistance to flow, resistance to the use of the dimensional structure and its communicative possibilities brought through a clear reflection of the 6th dimensional grid system.

If there is a lot of cellulite there is almost always a blockage to accepting the divine blueprint, either not recognizing its availability, not able to access it, or perhaps a more intricate pattern of resistance which would have to be individually interpreted by me for you. I'm going to develop a program which will give each of you an analysis of the use of the dimensions. It will become available through Tibetan Foundation channels soon. If you are interested in such an analysis you may write to the Foundation and ask for it. It will cover those things which I find important to give you in how you are able to use a multi-dimensional approach and those areas in which I find important resistances. It seems to me that our dimensional work together is one of the most important tools to aid raising of consciousness on your planet.

CHAPTER 5

USING DIMENSIONAL TOOLS TO DEVELOP OPPORTUNITIES

We continue now with our discussion of the dimensions. As you begin to discover what dimensions are you will find that there is an inner excitement, literally, which presents itself to you. It will be rather like finally having found an opening which gives you the whole layout or a tool to penetrate and understand how to create whatever you seek to create in your life. There are many specific ways to use your new found dimensional understanding as a very practical tool in your life. This is not a "far-out" esoteric discussion we are having but perhaps we have needed some conceptual understanding of it and then some practice to allow the concepts to be recognized as practical tools.

Let us say that you have a new opportunity and you know that that opportunity is something that will be helpful in your life. What can you do to ensure that you will use that opportunity wisely and well? Let us here look at several hypothetical situations and in each one I will give you a flow of dimensional contacts which will enhance your opportunity. Now there is some generalization here but these examples apply to most of you most of the time. There is a means to generalize dimensional flow and that is through the Earth contact. I want to go into this a little before we begin to give you the examples.

First then, your Earth is approaching the 4th dimension but that is its point of realization which is being approached. It does not mean that the Earth is being confined only to the use of the 4th dimension. It will continue to interact with the 3rd and certainly the 5th and the 6th. We could say what it is doing is communicating with those parts of itself which are already functioning on these other dimensions.

Again, as before, I tell you that these are alternate realities. The Earth then in its greater and clearer understanding of alternate realities or possibilities is allowing a conceptual framework within which you can function and take advantage of opportunities which "parallel" the Earth's experience. Because of the nature of the 4th dimensions, for the next 20 to 25 years (this is being written in the fall of 1988) the flow or all of what the 4th dimension represents is being emphasized on your Earth.

There will be rapid change, rapid progression of communication. There will be a need to let go, to release quickly because the next opportunity or the next contact within the present opportunity will be flowing to you. It is important to see that communication is the key for living now. There are times when one goes out and communicates, there are times when one integrates what has already been communicated. This is an outreach of communication that your Earth is presently emphasizing. What is meant here is that the overall learning within the Earth's mass consciousness is one of communication, outreach, becoming aware of yourself through sharing with others, becoming aware of your soul's overall purpose, becoming aware of how to link together, becoming aware of light, the body of light - the use of your light potential. In a previous volume I have given many light techniques to allow you to expand your understanding of yourself as light, to wear your light in an ever more comprehensive manner.

The Earth in its communication is linking into other aspects of itself, flowing if you will, its consciousness into contact with those aspects, allowing a clearer understanding within itself at this doorway of the 4th dimension and with those other parts of itself that it contacts. You too then have an opportunity to get in touch with all aspects of self on every level, from every point of view. Now we may call these other aspects alternate realities or we may call them the 4-body system. The point is that all aspects of who you really are can now flow to a clearer, more integrated understanding and thus be used as an ingredient for fulfilling your reason for being here on the Earth.

Believe me, your soul is aware of the opportunities that await you, that are here now. You cannot escape from them - they will follow you even if you try to resist them - isn't that interesting? Opportunity is there and if you flow with it, it will be "easy", if you do not it may be "difficult" but the opportunities are there in either case. Your Earth is truly in its consciousness a combination of all of the kingdoms that use it as a "home" base and incoming links of consciousness which are universal in nature on many levels and from many points of view. It is now a particularly potent learning point to understand the 4th dimension. <u>In the Earth school what is being emphasized now, is how to make contact with and communicate with opportunities.</u> Also then how to flow within them, how to use them well. And these are not necessarily what you may consider only esoteric opportunities, they can be spiritually stimulating and connecting but opportunities to get into a basic connection with who you are and how then to partake of the opportunity which is offered through understanding who you are.

Let us now go into some examples where one can use a clearer dimensional understanding to assist you with what may be coming up for you in the next few months and certainly within the next few years.

Example Of Connecting Into And Energizing The Opportunity You Seek

I want to show you this very effective method of energizing an opportunity for yourself through this following example: You are a teacher, but you are aware that you are not yet using your abilities fully. In fact, although you are already welltrained in your field you are considering further training in order to advance your opportunities and to allow a satisfaction in the job area. It doesn't matter if this is an esoteric type of teaching or a more traditional role within the school system or even a rather informal type of teaching with friends. How can you then use the dimensions?

Seek to see that you have already a solid foundation to move into a wider and more comprehensive way of teaching. Try to sense that being upon the Earth has already provided a firm basis within which to move up the ladder of awareness as far as your teaching abilities and getting more and more opportunities are concerned. That basis is already there.

You are very experienced in the use of the 3rd dimension. You have used it from every point of view, therefore all that is needed is to use that well defined, secure foundation in a manner that flows multi-dimensionally. That is the key - the multi-dimensional use which includes the 3rd dimension. You have worn the 3rd dimension as you would a very comfortable basic garment that you can now evolve or beautify through adding other components to it so that your whole "light outfit" is enhanced.

See yourself then comfortable in the 3rd dimension. For some of you, you will need to clear material which says, "I don't want to be here physically." What you're really saying is you don't want to be in the 3rd dimension. You do enjoy the 4th and many of you the 5th and certainly the 6th. The 3rd dimension is not "the bad guy." It just has not yet been clearly understood or even clearly defined.

4th Dimension. Again you have a good basic understanding of it. You have emotionally accepted the 4th dimension and that is extremely important. The 4th dimension is the natural home for your emotional body, remember, and once your emotional body accepts a format there is a movement, a flow which becomes natural and easy to use. So as you seek to flow into this teaching opportunity you could see the 3rd dimension foundation secure but floating on a movement, perhaps a river. The 3rd dimension could be a raft, not a boat, a solid, sturdy, wide raft which you are on. Now, this raft will not tip over. It goes up and down with the flow and it is moved by that flow easily, steered easily. It has almost an irrepressible movement, there's no way that foundation can get stuck or caught. It is moving and there is no way to stop it. If you can sense that your teaching opportunity is fundamentally strong and well developed and now upon the flow which is drawing you irresistibly into the opportunity that you are seeking this is the means to unite your skills, your abilities with what you want.

<u>The 5th dimension.</u> Here are building blocks of your understanding and what I would like you to do is to see various building blocks upon your raft. Now they are very practicable in that you can construct shelter, a place to sleep, a bed, a chair, and a means of elevating your view. You can build up through these building blocks a means to become higher on your raft so you can see very well and yet they are very sturdy, very reliable. They need to be together. There are a number of them. They need to be integrated and you might begin to see them in various geometric shapes and see what they represent to you in the case of teaching opportunities. There may be one that represents communication, there may be another that represents security, there may be one that represents integration. Each building block is a strength that you have or that you feel you need to achieve your goal. Some strengths are listed below and you may think of many others needed for your goal. After you have selected your strengths, your building blocks six to ten of them, move the building blocks around. Ask yourself, "in what way can I put them together to construct a clearer contact with the higher energies of my soul and its purposes?" Your greater and greater understanding will invoke from doing so a contact with the 6th dimension.

A NON-INCLUSIVE LIST OF STRENGTHS
(To be used with the heart qualities)

Aligned
Available
Balanced
Channeling Ability
Communication Skills
Conceptual
Confident
Courageous
Creative
Dedicated
Dependable
Dynamic
Experienced
Generosity
Helpful
Ingenious
Inspiring
Integrated
Knowledgeable
Magnetic
Open
Optimistic
Patient
Perservering
Receptive
Responsible
Secure
Self-Disciplined
Service-Oriented
Skilled appropriately
Supportive
Thorough
Understanding
Well-educated

As your are moving the concepts, the building blocks, the strengths around, you will sense an almost electrical quality in your processing. There is an excitement generated that infuses the movement of the concepts, they seem to move easily, automatically without stress or strain and they seem to create a light surge which is generating the energy which draws you irresistibly along this 4th dimensional flow. This is your contact with the 6th dimension.

The 6th Dimension. We talk about it in many ways and it is yet a little difficult for some of you to understand what it really is. I have said it is the divine blueprint which has been reflected from the 9th dimension so that physicality may use the divine blueprint more easily and more clearly. We could call it an energizer, an integrator, a connector, a simplifier, a relaxer, depending upon your various bodies and how they contact it. It many times relaxes the physical body. It connects with the emotional body, it electrifies the mental body and, of course, it creates a foundation for the spiritual body through connecting it to all of the various formats or dimensions.

It is important then to recognize that in your teaching goal that visualization can be the first step to opportunity. After using the visualization, the next step is to be aware enough to notice the opportunity when it comes in. It may not come in your "old" manner. It is necessary to be creative, to see opportunities now on the Earth. One way in which opportunities may come in is through your clearer recognition that you may expect opportunities and therefore your willingness to invoke them. In other words, you may seek opportunities a "little" more assertively. Now that does not mean that you must go every place physically as you may have done in the past, seeking a job for example. It does mean that if you get a glimpse of a possibility you may want to pursue it more actively than you would have before. Why? Because you have, through this visualization, been invoking an opportunity and you want to be sure you don't let go of it before you've contacted it completely.

By that I mean that for some of you, although you may be doing quite well in your visualization you may not have energized it completely yet. However you may have strengths which begin to manifest it and you can contact it at the beginning by seeing some possibilities and pursuing them until you can decide if those possibilities are an opportunity that you wish to pursue further.

As you keep working with your visualization, and I would do it once a day and for perhaps ten minutes to begin with and when you have an odd moment you might energize it. Keep moving your building blocks around, keep working with the concept area so that it will energize for you the higher qualities of the heart. That's the key to manifesting opportunities. The qualities of the heart:

110

receptivity, allowingness, trust, gratitude, joy, unconditional love, appreciation, serenity, humility, charm, loyalty, adaptibility, wisdom, honesty, and clarity. Will all manifest in your life through the choice area, through surrendering to the soul and through the discernment of such opportunities. I promise you this: if you keep working to build a strong visualization for an opportunity you desire it will create opportunities for you, more than one and in more than one way.

There is one further powerful visualization using the heart qualities that you may add to this if you wish. Now it is very powerful so before you do it be certain that you really want such an opportunity, because, my friend, this will almost insure it unless there are individual circumstances which in a subconscious sense create a huge blocking of the energy, of flowing into this opportunity. As I view humanity and those who will read this volume, less than one percent of you have such overwhelming blocks within the subconscious.

This then is the addition to your visualization: find an arrangement of your building blocks, your strengths, which seems to invoke the electrical flow of the 6th dimension very clearly. One way to know this is that your visualization may just seem to move more rapidly. There's a flow in it as never before. Don't try this until you've worked with this visualization for a while, my friends. Now when its really moving well there is a rapid electrical content to your flow. Now on a piece of paper draw your raft, the river and your geometric shapes, your 6 to 10 building blocks of strengths that have fit together in such a way that they create this electrical contact. You may have squares, rectangles and triangles, you may have hexagon's, but each building block is a particular integrative concept. Now, the important step, using your knowingness to determine what qualities of the heart each block represents, and writing down on the building block itself that quality - one per building block. Even if you get several qualities as you seek to define one, choose the one which seems to have the most energy in it. Look at it in your knowingness, which is more electric as you associate it with the building block? You may see it as iridescent, as luminous, as sparking. Look for the electrical content. Remember, this will work the best for you when those building blocks are sparking completely. They are very electrified and they are flowing the raft toward the goal in a very electrical manner.

Write down on your building blocks the qualities of the heart that you have chosen. Now when you are doing this is the time, my friends, to really go into and understand conceptually what each of these qualities of the heart mean to you. Discuss them with your friends, read about them, read the following material about each quality of the heart. The heart directly accesses a free-flowing creativity. Indeed creativity cannot flow freely without coming through the heart. An expansive expression allows the heart to gain a sense of being included in your creativity.

By that I mean that if one does not use the qualities of the heart very much there is a sense of separation built into the creative process. The emotional body then doesn't "get the message", doesn't make the desired link into unlimited level of creativity which you are seeking.

We are listing in this section specific heart qualities but remember there must be a willingness to enter heart territory in relation to your creativity. Put another way, what I am saying is that you can't hold on to your creativity without sharing it because creativity never expresses alone. It is always shared even if one is physically alone while expressing it there are emotional and spiritual connections, and sometimes mental and conceptual as well.

Creativity in its fullest sense is often stretched, expanded through the specific progressional responses of the heart. In this material I'm going to give you a list of qualities of the heart which is comprehensive but not all inclusive. If you get others then please write them down but also make sure that you ask yourself what you understand about each of these qualities.

The first one I bring to you is :

<u>JOY:</u> the ability to allow life to be freely experienced and comprehensively shared. Movement is always emphasized. Joy bubbles from deeply within the heart. Joy's expression is the basic divine quality and the prime motivator for existence itself. It permits alignment, it permits integration, it permits flow, it permits literally a whole divine expression.

<u>UNCONDITIONAL LOVE:</u> the ability to connect without judgment, without resistance, without reservation. The means to share all divine qualities. Love is the ultimate flow connector. It is the electrical expression of Source, the magnetic electrical connector or Sourceness itself. It completes, it expands, it creates unity, ends any sense of separation, releases barriers. This allows full communication.

<u>GRATITUDE:</u> is the means by which one opens to possibilities because gratitude allows those possibilities to come in. It acknowledges your interconnection with all that is and your interdependance with all else in the Whole. Gratitude releases unworthiness, self-centeredness, inability to connect, barriers, indeed gratitude is the ultimate key to the expansion of the heart and all of its qualities.

<u>TRUST:</u> I have written extensively about trust. In this capsule comment it is a connector, it is the means to bridge seeming

impossible or unknown qualities, it allows the emotional body to connect into one's potential. It opens communicative possibilities between those that do not yet understand each other well. Through trust one bridges racial barriers, ethnic barriers, age barriers, social/political barriers. All barriers can be released through trust, trusting the divine process, trusting something greater, bridging to it through trust.

RECEPTIVITY: being open would be the capsule definition of receptivity but the openess interconnects with many other qualities of the heart and it stimulates the process of evolution. Openness or receptivity is as clear as your experiences have allowed it to be but not necessarily physical experiences. Receptivity is connected to your Source level relationship. The basic meaning of receptivity then is to be open to the unlimited expression of your divine beingness.

ALLOWINGNESS: certainly we could talk about allowingness as we have receptivity but perhaps we will also say that allowingness is the outreach of receptivity. Often it allows a connection with others into their point of view, into what they are receptive to. It also is a connector in the fullest sense but it allows others their choices as well as self. It allows you to choose what you are receptive to and what you wish to create. Allowingness is an investment in viewing the process and learning from it.

APPRECIATION: certainly also relates to gratitude but appreciation also relates to a quality that you may wish to identify separately. It's called wonder, but could be a part of appreciation which is where I am putting it. The wonder of existence is truly a miraculous contact with the heart. One appreciates the plan, appreciates the gift of the plan, appreciates the Creator, appreciates life itself, appreciates the Earth, appreciates other people's efforts, appreciates opportunities, literally the wonder of existence comes in and manifests appreciation.

SERENITY: also one might put in here stability which I consider to be a part of the heart and you may want to use it for serenity on one of your building blocks. Serenity contains allowingness and gratitude, many other qualities are built into it but it is a point of knowingness where life is really allowed - appreciated - discovered - treasured and unfolded without imbalance, without an overly expressed point of view. It has a connotation of flow which is allowed to be stable and divinely inspired. Inspiration, although I am not giving it a separate category, is another heart quality which I find an important part of serenity.

HUMILITY: this is a very important heart quality that I've talked about a great deal. I consider it to be the ability to see divine equality, that you are not less-than, that others are not either more-than or less-than. You see that all is equal and that you may

116

express that equality without straining through the ego needs because you've seen how you fit in and you feel humble, not again less-than but aware of the magnificence and truly expanding nature of the divine plan, you recognize also that your part in it need not be forced upon the attention of others. Humility creates the communicative link that evens out the barriers which challenge your ability to perceive clearly. Humility, then, is a key in the communication between the mental and emotional perspective whether in your self or in others.

CHARM: You may be surprised to have this included in our heart qualities. Many times it is equated with the personality level. However, I truly believe there is nothing more charming than the Source, the Divine as it sparkles creating a truly magnificent and magnetic effect. Many of you are drawn to those great teachers who have sought to motivate, to assist you. They use this quality of charm to do so. It is an invocational quality which invites a sharing process because one cannot resist it. Charm is not manipulative but so sparkling, refreshing and invigorating that one joins with it just to experience the "charm" of it. There are, of course, non-clear levels of charm but in the clearest sense of its use it is an important heart quality used to motivate and attract others to a clearer point of view.

LOYALTY: There are several qualities that fit together here. I have chosen loyalty as one that expresses as a connector to something that one finds worth being loyal to. In the sense that we are discussing let us say that something worth being loyal to is the Divine Plan. On the human level loyalty sometimes seems to close doors. On the Divine level it opens them. Because what you are loyal to is the ever expanding communicative link system which we call "The Plan." Through conscious awareness that you are within this plan all of the time and that it speaks to you and through you by means of the co-creator system, then your loyalty to that system opens a sense of being supported by all of what you are being loyal to, humanity, the teachers, the co-creators and the creator.

ADAPTABILITY/FLEXIBILITY: allows input into your understanding, allows you to change your mind, to benefit from others understanding, to gain an integrative perspective through your willingness to change. Your understanding and acceptance of change are perhaps the major key to your evolution. By letting go of rigidity through recognizing that you can have input from others you remove barriers and sometimes confusion. This is such an important area that I encourage you to keep exploring it.

WISDOM: this is certainly a heart quality. It is divine proportion from a heart perspective. It literally oversees the use of all heart qualities. How much humility, how much trust, how much receptivity, how much allowingness should one use as one functions within the co-creator process in partnership with humanity? Knowing the answer to this is true wisdom. Wisdom knows the balancing which uses all heart qualities through a conceptual strength that penetrates into Divine Beingness. It is not really attached to doingness. One is wise, then, to allow the Divine to appear more clearly even when there does not seem to be an immediate need to refer to it.

HONESTY: honesty is a perspective of stripping away levels of illusion. Each person can only be honest with themselves by getting rid of such illusion and thus they are able to share the honesty with others. Honesty then, a relative point to each, depending upon the amount of illusion or confusion which still exists in a subconscious sense.

CLARITY: clarity is an integrative point, therefore it belongs in the heart area. The Source is clear, therefore it is completely integrated. Your clarity depends upon your understanding, it depends upon your level of honesty with yourself, it depends upon your wisdom, it depends literally upon all factors which you search and research in order to keep evolving that level called clarity. The ability to be clear is the ability to understand your Source level perspective which is virtually unlimited.

KINDNESS: is an opening to the needs of others in humanity, a willingness to respond , to communicate and to aid them even if it is not within your "comfort factor." It is perhaps one outpouring of unconditional love that can be recognized on all levels and in all aspects of life experience.

As I said at the beginning of this section, these are not all of the qualities of the heart. Of course not, but I have given you a cross-section of them to spark your own creativity, to help you expand into a clearer contact with those areas which are importantly a part of these building blocks. Try to find a word, a heart quality, that results in an expression of the electric effect when you label your building block with it. You might lay joy over there. Does it expand a lot? Do rockets go off literally electrically? Keep laying words on the blocks until you get an expanding effect. There may be several possibilities and you may have to try one and then try another and see which expansion is the greatest. Remember, I advised between six and ten building blocks and one heart quality to a block.

Now, as you are laying in the final one keep working with it. There may be, in a few cases, one quality that may be used twice. Unconditional love may possibly, for about ten percent of you, be used more than once. Also receptivity and clarity. It will depend upon your beliefs about these qualities. Do not, I repeat, do not put more than one quality on one of these building blocks. It will simply confuse the issue.

Now, as you are putting in the last one, you're looking for, literally, an explosive effect. You're looking for an effect where a skyrocket goes off electrically. You may have to keep working with it a while, keep putting them in until it literally explodes, but not negatively, a creative explosion that takes you to this next level of creativity and what you may see through this explosion is a visualization of really moving to that next level. You sail through that door of opportunity. Or there may be another way, you may be drawn up higher into a rocket-like effect and then take off.

Whatever your symbol, you are looking for a key to expanding the creativity so that the last component, the last quality that you put into your building blocks should be the one that generates that movement that you're looking for.

Now, if you don't get this effect right away, don't be discouraged. You simply need to look at the qualities. Remember now, as you put each one in, you're going to study it and it may be if you're not getting your electrical explosion then you haven't studied the qualities enough to have developed a clear understanding of them. So keep studying the qualities of the heart and it may be that you're in the right ballpark with the quality but you don't have it worded just right. We talked about certain qualities like wonder and appreciation that are united in a sense and you need to express them just a little differently. So keep working with it. Use the dictionary, and talk to your friends - as I said, look in books. Find out what these qualities mean to you. Ask your four bodies - what do these qualities mean? Discuss the qualities of the heart until when you place them on your building blocks there will be this tremendous electrical expansion and that my friends is the opening that you're looking for. I'm talking about an expansion with so much life force in it that it moves very dramatically and quickly to a new level. Well, that truly is exciting and I thank you very much.

I want to give you several other examples in invoking opportunities with life itself. Getting in touch with your soul's purposes may be one opportunity that you all are interested in. Remember that there is never a single purpose but multiple or expanding purposes. Use the same foundation within the 3rd dimension as in the previous exercise. Certainly use the raft within the 4th dimension, the river - the flow. Instead of seeing the building blocks on the raft - see them on the shore and as your raft passes them you can reach out with your arm or with some sort of a hook and bring them in, and then look at them clearly and see what quality of the heart you're holding. I would suggest that as you bring them in from the shore, each one, that you hold it in your arms and you actually rock it as you would a baby and then look at that lovely child - is it serenity? Is it wisdom? Is it trust? Is it joy? Is it unconditional love? Whatever it is, sit and hold it until you can identify it and then from the point of view of your purposes seek to understand that quality.

You know I could go through these qualities now and give you more meaning from your purpose point of view, the ability to trust will be the ability to know that your purpose is flowing, is moving and that you can connect with it. But you, yourself, can go through this list and see as you nurture - that's another heart quality that we didn't talk about - but see as you nurture that building block that you've been able to grasp as you flowed along on your raft, your foundation, that you've now built a relationship with this strength, this strength that the building block represents.

It's there and you're nurturing it and as you bring on board now up to ten of these qualities, these building blocks, that what will occur is more and more unity within them. Each time you bring one in you nurture it until you know its quality then place it with the others that you've already brought on board. See how they interrelate and you might have to work with them a little, communicate with them a little. Tell each one that you're placing it now with your other strengths. Tell it to communicate. Help it if it needs help or, if it feels a little strange coming into this new format. Introduce it - say to gratitude "I want to introduce you to joy." Say to gratitude "I want to introduce you to humility - they're here already. Get acquainted with them - communicate with them now." And thus in this exercise again what you're looking for is that point where you've put in enough qualities - maybe up to ten - where again there is this tremendous electrical surge. Use the 6th dimension as the sparking connection also used in the previous exercise. The only difference in this exercise is the way that you gather up the building blocks which represent the qualities of the heart. As you allow your strengths into the flow of your purposes look for the next level of connection which will be ignited as those strengths become integrated within this flow of your life which is the flow of your purposes here on the Earth.

Try to be truly creative about this basic exercise putting in any sort of an opportunity that you are trying to create and using the acquisition of the building blocks in different ways. If you aren't making a connection at all with an opportunity you may find the building blocks rather hidden and you have to go in search for them and there may be an area where you find one within a swamp, underneath the swampy conditions there, and you have to figure out how to get it out. What symbolically are you learning? If you can't find your building blocks in any sort of a scenario then say to your knowingness, "alright connect me with where they are - give me a symbolic way to recognize them that I may learn from it." Another example is you may find them in a church, in a cathedral, you may find them in a football stadium, you may find them in a pharmacy, you may find them in a hospital, you may find them in a beautiful field of flowers, you may find them in the mountains or at the seashore. Look at the symbols given there - unite with them and see what they represent to you - understand that as clearly as possible.

Alright, good. You will need to ask that building block what quality it is and then your understanding of how you rescued it or brought it into your life will help you to integrate what it represents into the purposeful reason for why you want this opportunity now.

CHAPTER 6

GENERATING DIMENSIONAL EXPERIENCES

EXERCISE: See a corridor and it is emerald green. On the right of it are three doors and on the left of it are five doors. See yourself walking the corridor, now the doors are closed and you walk from one end to the other and back gathering up a sense of energy within the corridor. You're becoming familiar with the energy in the corridor. Go back and forth in the corridor walking in this emerald green energy until you sense a buoyancy from that energy and you no longer are walking in contact with the "floor" but you begin to rise in the corridor. The corridor has no upper limit - no ceiling - you walk it then back and forth until you can sense that you are walking at least six feet above the floor. Now don't go up more than ten feet. You might want to have a gauge between six feet and ten feet so that you know when you've entered that range. Now I'd like you to practice swimming in the emerald green energy in that six to ten foot range. Now, swim back and forth until it feels easy, it flows well, its rather like swimming in a beautiful emerald green sea. Practice various strokes if you will, the breaststroke, the backstroke, whatever you wish until there is a proficiency in your swimming style. Its very easy to go back and forth the whole corridor from the starting point to the turning around point which is the end of a corridor. The corridor then is used as a means of actively utilizing your conscious awareness, moving it easily and freely from one point to another.

When you feel the freedom of movement then back at the starting point I would like you to swim to one of the doors. Remember there are three and five doors. Choose one on either side and swim to it and open it. Now the goal is to see what is behind that door, to choose whether to enter it and if you do enter it see what sort of an experience you will have. Now, remember your emerald green energy in the corridor. It won't spill out as you open the door, let's not create that, but remember it is the connector between each of the doors and you may need after experiencing one door to come out in your corridor and swim back and forth until there is again an ease of movement. Use the corridor then as the flow that connects you multi-dimensionally. Each of the doors represents for you a particular dimensional experience. It may be that you have several on the 3rd dimension, it may be that you have only one or two on the 4th dimension, it may be that you have perhaps none on the 5th dimensions, it doesn't really matter - the point is to have the dimension experience behind a door and then go back to your corridor and swim back and forth - go then to the next door - enter it and see what sort of an experience you have. Use all eight doors in this manner. Be sure that you write down the type of experience that lies awaiting you behind each door, write down whether you choose to be in that experience and then after you have completed all eight I would like you to swim back and forth in your corridor until you understand how all eight fit together.

The back and forth movement in the corridor symbolically represents the flow that connects all these dimensional experiences. Remember - if subconsciously you are trying to understand one dimension rather completely you might have seven of these doors relating to that one dimension. It is not meant that you direct yourself to see each door as a different dimension. It is meant that you should allow your subconscious - your creativity - to bring you an experience behind each door that needs to be interrelated to a flow, to an evolving understanding and also to an ability to integrate various facets of a dimension. What I'm saying here is perhaps the 5th dimension is one that many of you need to understand more clearly. It relates, as we've stated before in this volume to the mental perspective on two levels but especially on the conceptual level. There are many aspects of that dimension that need to be understood and perhaps several of your doors will give you a certain aspect of the 5th dimension that need to be interrelated with other aspects of that dimension as well as seeing how all of the 5th dimension in its integrated state fits in with other dimensions.

This exercise can be done as simply or as comprehensively as you wish and we could also look at it as a spiral, meaning that you could go into your doors, interrelate them on one level and then again by going back and forth in your flow move the whole experience to another level, go into your doors again, again interrelate them through the emerald energy corridor and then complete that level of the spiral. There can be as many as you wish or simply one in which you seek to understand how a certain experience has a dimensional focus.

Perhaps one of the most important points about this exercise is this: it teaches you to see what dimensions you are functioning in, in every experience that you have. Let us say that you enter a door, for example, and the angels are sitting around on beautiful rocks playing golden harps, the rocks are iridescent and there are clouds for the floor. Now as you step into it you begin to recognize that you're no longer in a physical dimension, that indeed you've gone beyond the 6th dimension into this 7th dimensional focus where the angels function and live. I would say that for most of you the subconscious mind will seek to give you either a very practical, everyday situation so that you can see how it relates dimensionally or a spiritual experience so that you can integrate that into the flow, the emerald corridor of your physical experience.

You will remember that I told you to have a gauge in the corridor between six and ten feet is where you want to swim. If you find yourself swimming sixty feet above the base of your corridor you will no longer be in contact with physical existence. It is not appropriate in our exercise that you allow your spiritual aspirations to pull you from the physical dimensions that you have chosen to learn in. The point of our exercise is to relate each dimensional experience, whether or not it seems physically oriented such as our angel example, to your learning on the physical level.

In our example of the angel experience you would need to interrelate it to the other experiences in the other seven doors and see how the angels were playing an important part in either teaching you, supporting you, or allowing you to make certain contacts with a clearer life on the physical level. The goal of this exercise is to integrate your understanding of those points that seem perhaps not yet clear in the use of the dimensions, to flow them together through the emerald green corridor.

If there is one door experience that doesn't seem to have anything to do with anything - you can't integrate it - then look at your gauge - see you are swimming between six and ten feet - swim back and forth - swim back and forth - back and forth - back and forth and as you do consider that room, then consider the room next to it and the relationship to it - swim back and forth, move it back and forth, keep swimming back and forth and if you keep doing this you will integrate that seemingly unrelated experience into the others. It may take you more than one attempt, you may want to say as you go to sleep at night: " I want to swim in the emerald green corridor and I want to, on the inner planes, seek to understand how this experience fits into the other. I also direct my subconscious to receive any dreams that will help me in this important integrative process."

Good, you can use this as extensively as you wish. You could also use it on a group basis with multiples of eight, having one person, behind each door, really represent that experience so you would interact with a particular person rather than going into a room and seeing what was there. You would open your door and find there the person, one of eight, communicate with them, they would mirror back to you through communication something they felt was important for you to know. They would attune to you in this exercise. You would then see yourself swimming at their vibrational rate.

You could even use a swimming pool itself on the physical level. Certainly that would not be the way most of you wanted to do it but if someone wishes and has the swimming pool handy - why not? Remember to swim in water that is from six to ten feet. That is the important point. So be creative but use the doors as an indicator of what needs to be integrated into a clearer use of the dimensions.

The Golden Elevator

EXERCISE: You have a golden elevator. Now the golden elevator will go wherever you need to go to clarify your understanding dimensionally. When you want to clarify your understanding of a particular dimension you may consciously direct the elevator to that area. Let us say, for example, you do not yet understand the 5th dimension. Get on your elevator, push five, go to that level, get off and see what awaits you there. Now you will want to keep a piece of paper handy or a tape recorder and either write down or record what occurs in this opening through your golden elevator. Write down the detail that is there, everything that you see or know because you can do these exercises, of course, through your knowingness as well as your clairvoyant abilities. You can also do them through the feeling nature or the sensing nature which is a part of your physical body.

Alright, learn then from your golden elevator which will take you to a particular floor that you direct it to. The other way to use the golden elevator is to say to it: "I don't know - it seems to me that there are points I am not clear in dimensionally but I don't know where they are - please take me to where they are." And you allow the elevator to again bring you into contact with a point of non-clarity in your dimensional understanding. Again, get off your elevator and record, either on a piece of paper or a tape recorder what you see or what you know about this inner experience. This would work well in a group also. If there is, for example, a group of six people, one could say to their golden elevator: "allow this group to portray for me through a type of a role playing, a type of a play, something that I need to understand dimensionally." Then it is important to visualize or know that you are getting on the elevator and moving into contact with that point of view. All of the group will want to attune to that process, bring it into focus and then bring such a play or communication to you. Actually this could be done on groups of any size from two to literally two hundred or even larger, however, the larger groups might want to break up into smaller groups.

CHAPTER 7

HOOKING INTO A MULTI-DIMENSIONAL MODE OF EXPERIENCING

It is important, my friends, to keep learning about dimensions, to keep asking yourself: "what do I understand now from what Vywamus has brought to me about dimensions? What are dimensions and how am I using them?" Look daily at your life. When you get up be sure you are always focused in the 3rd dimension. When you are waking up there needs to be an adjustment and attunement process. It is very difficult for your physical structure and for your consciousness if you leap out of bed. You may experience a sense of disorientation because you are not allowing yourself to be stabilized in that 3rd dimension that is the foundation for your outer experience. If you leap up before you have stabilized it many times you do not "hook-in" the multi-dimensional flow in a way that you can use it clearly during that day and for that reason your day may become confusing, disorganized or out of sync and it takes the night and the inner experience to again realign the use of the dimensional flow. Or realignment can be established through a period of meditation or a period of relaxation of some kind.

The point is, it only takes about five minutes after you wake up to allow that structure to be stabilized multi-dimensionally. It's like landing "plop" in the 3rd dimension. Now you need to stand up and balance, take a deep breath, and see where you are besides where your feet are. Then "hook-in" all of the other dimensions and then when they are securely "fastened in" you begin to flow multi-dimensionally.

This can be important also when you change types of activity. Let us say that you are attending a very mental lecture or in your job as a scientist, a computer analyst, a teacher, you are using the 5th dimension rather completely, the mental body is directing your activity. Now when you get very focused into one dimension, no matter what it is, you need again an adjustment period, an adjustment process when you widen your perspective, or again allow yourself to flow multi-dimensionally.

Let us say that you've been reading some very scientific material or something that exercised your mental body, studying perhaps, learning for about an hour. When you are finished with that visualize yourself plugging in again multi-dimensionally. Certainly the exercise I gave your earlier about the emerald green corridor and the flowing in it is a good one to use to connect you with all dimensional possibilities and opportunities.

You might, then, at the end of your intense 5th dimensional/mental activity of an hour swim again in your emerald green corridor until you can sense a connection beyond the one that you have been focused on. If, however, your activity has been in the music, the arts, the dance fields, at the end of that period you might want to, as you flow in your corridor, go and stand in all eight doorways, seeing that you can make a connection eight different ways. Now at this point the eight does not represent eight dimensions but eight, the number eight is a power number and it will literally empower you to focus wherever you wish and to combine various dimensions into a multi-flowing experience.

<u>Eventually</u> my friends even if you are intensely focused in one dimension you will still be able to consciously utilize the other dimensions also. This is perhaps, for most of you, a ways in your future. It is the ability to use the 4th dimension as a projector into all points of view simultaneously. This is what we, on your spiritual plane, can do well. You can learn to do it also but for most of you there needs to be yet a rather focused approach to dimensions at times using sequential time as a focus which helps you learn and grow.

If you seek to plug-in multi-dimensionally beyond sequential time too soon what you get is a sense of confusion and disorientation. I would say then allow yourself to focus in to one dimension and learn from it but recognize that as you learn to connect multi-dimensionally there will come a time when your multi-dimensional expression is not disturbed or taken away by your learning process.

You sometimes experience, or at least some of you, a drain of energy from concentration into one dimension. You then may feel fatigued or tired because of this concentration. Particularly for many of you of the mental body. The reason is this: you literally have placed all of your eggs in one basket and you are not feeding energy into the physical, emotional or sometimes the spiritual perspective or body. What this means is that the energy structure which is your auric field can become depleted in the sense that you are actively utilizing only one part of it for rather prolonged periods of time.

If you go to a healer and they tell you your four body energy structure is out of alignment, almost always this is caused by an over-concentration upon one of the bodies without allowing energy connections with the other bodies.

There is a rather simple remedy to this that will keep your energy structure, your auric field in greater alignment because of course your fourbodies each have an energy perspective which come together to make up your auric field.

There is also, beside the four bodies, the etheric or energy storage level which closely surrounds your physical body. Thus we are looking at the etheric, the energy storage system, which could be related to the physical body storage structure, the emotional body's energy structure, the mental body's energy structure and the spiritual body's energy structure.

Now some people will say there is a fifth and certainly there is, and it is the integration or the overall energy structure. If then you are focused for a mental activity intensely, without moving around, without using your emotions, without spiritual input you, in one sense, shut off the communication energy-wise between the segments or parts of your auric field. It gets then out of balance because of an overactivity in the mental structure, a movement mentally that cannot be followed or aligned with the emotional, physical and spiritual because there is no, at that point, bridging of the energy. There is no multi-dimensional flow bridges being made. It is common for humanity to use only one part of their energy and then not know how to interrelate or integrate that energy to allow the other parts of their energy bodies to benefit by the activity whether it be physical, emotional, mental or spiritual. I would suggest as you go into any type of activity that you do the following:

Briefly visualize your physical body, see surrounding it, for most of you, about a quarter to a half an inch the etheric storage system, the energy system of your physical body. View it as very bright. You don't need to scan it individually, but view your physical figure as surrounded by a bright energy that flames forth and is generally clear in color. Now see your aura connecting beyond where it is and still following the outline of the physical structure because, my friends, although this is not exactly the way your aura is I want you to relate it to the physical structure because we are emphasizing the learning within physicality.

See then your emotional body's energy surrounding the etheric storage system of your physical body. Now it can be any color that talks to you of emotion. I'll give you a suggestion but if you wish to use another color certainly do so. My suggestion is to see then beyond this rather clear energy of the etheric structure an emerald green energy. Let us generalize the size of it for the purpose of this exercise and see it about three inches wide all around the physical body as evenly as possible. What you are doing here is for the purpose of this exercise only. It is not the way the auric field is really constructed, although there may be a few people who are using the aura more or less in this manner.

Beyond the beautiful three inch band of green representing your emotional body I'd like you to see a four inch band of golden yellow. Now the golden yellow is very vibrant. I would say iridescent. Beyond that golden yellow is a six inch band of violet that is again iridescent representing the spiritual body. So briefly use this visualization, before every activity that focuses you in one dimension or another, whether it be an exercise session which involves mostly the physical body, a dancing or artistic endeavor which may involve mostly the emotional body or perhaps a relationship experience or a mental endeavor involving mostly the mental body or even a spiritual experience such as meditation or transformational clearing or exercises. Then as you view the energy of the four body system be sure you see connections between the various energies.

I would suggest that you draw the aura that I have just described showing the clear, emerald green, yellow and violet around a physical figure.

Now the chakras are located as follows: the crown chakra - two or three inches above the head; the third eye chakra - in the vicinity just above the eyes and centered there; the throat chakra; the heart chakra; the solar plexus at their respective organ; the polarity at the sexual organs and base chakra at the base of the spine.

Now I would bridge from your drawing of the physical body to the outermost point of the violet which represents the spiritual body. Draw a bridge that connects because my friends this is where the connections are within the chakra system.

Now there are many, many, many more bridges. Really, specifically, there are ninety-nine bridges in your auric field but these seven are the main bridges. You might, however, in your knowingness, if one bridge for example at that sensitive point behind your ears seems important to you, then put a bridge there. If that sensitive point right in the shoulder area seems important put a bridge there but bridge it for all seven chakras and as you visualize the four body system and its energy, as you go into an experience see energy flowing to all four of these bodies into the structures that we are calling dimensions because that's what they are my friends, what holds your energy into the format of the four body system - this is what the dimensions are and by seeing them bridging you can allow, open up to, an energy exchange that allows you not to be drained, not to have your energy structure come out of alignment through certain rather intense activities that occur in your life.

Can you see how practical a tool this is? It doesn't even matter whether you know what activity, what dimensions your activity is focused on, you simply have to see the whole energy structure connected bridging, see energy flowing on it, you might even want to personify the energy, to see it as little people flowing back and forth, moving very busily and, my friends, you might want to take that into your physical structure, into the cellular level visualize all of your cells, which are seeds of universes, see bridges from the aura into all of the cells, every cell has an energy bridge and the energy is flowing back and forth between the cells.

Now it would be good to see this energy as an electrical flow but it can be people, it can be a color, and certainly you may vary the colors in any way that you wish. Use whatever symbolizes an energy flow to you.

CHAPTER 8

THE MULTI-DIMENSIONAL EARTH

As you gain a more complete understanding of what the dimensions are and begin to utilize that clearer understanding to aid your evolution, to aid your assisting others in their evolution each dimension becomes stronger. The reason is by focusing consciously and clearly into what these dimensions are and exploring them with greater and greater consciousness the structure of what they represent becomes lighter and the Earth itself evolves. It is interesting to note this.

One way of discussing the dimensions is to look at the ley lines or the grid system of your Earth. This grid system or these ley lines then surround the dense physical part of your Earth, they are the energy flow of the divine pattern of the Earth. They are indeed the energy structure of your Earth experience.

One can see then that there is an energy structure in connection with the 3rd dimension Earth, an energy structure in connection with the 4th dimension Earth, an energy structure in connection with the 5th dimension Earth, and an overlying or uniting energy structure in connection with the 6th dimension which allows a uniting of the other three perspectives. This is important because there are alternate realities my friends, there are other Earths and right now you are communicating with them much more than you yet know. It takes the soul level to reach the 6th dimension. I talked about this a little earlier in this volume but I want to go into it a little more comprehensively now from another point of view. Let me give you now an example.

Let us say that you have gone to school, grade school, high school, a university and perhaps graduate school and become a college professor. You practice your profession within the university but you have come up through the system learning in various other structures which were grade school, high school and college. You are able now within the university level to utilize the previous learning on all levels. You have gained, through your willingness to learn, a position which communicates and teaches from the college professor level.

Now you, as you read this, may have many, many points of view about college professors and I really don't want to get into that, but I am using this example as a demonstration of coming through the channels or progressing to a particular point where you have gathered up enough understanding. Your communication is now so valuable, is so clear that it utilizes all parts of what you have learned as a creative base that opens many, many doors of opportunity.

Now in our example of the college professor then it's necessary, I repeat, to look at it without getting into the Earth level learning of individual professors, to see what that level truly represents. In your present system it is considered the "highest" level of learning available in a formal sense and again I am merely using it as an example saying that this college professor represents here the 6th dimension which is guiding the progressive learning of others. The 6th dimension houses the "college professor" or your soul, that wise point of view that has for you at that level the ideal way for you to live your life. It is wise, loving, understanding and comprehensively "educated" so it understands the system or the structure.

Now going back to our college professor analogy, the college professor may have students that are freshmen, some that are sophomores, juniors, seniors and graduate students, this is not always true, but in our example this is certainly possible. He or she is then communicating with different levels of learning which are carefully structured as far as the curriculum is concerned, a graded type of structure which seeks in a step by step manner to allow the student to gain greater and greater understanding of what is being studied. Now your soul is of course a much greater college professor than any physical one having comprehensive and basic knowledge of the ideal manner in which you can live your life and how you may assist humanity and the

Earth to be a loving, peaceful, communicative center.

I'd like to have you consider then that the 3rd, the 4th, and the 5th dimensional Earths are points of view which are there already physically and your soul perspective focused on the 6th dimension is seeking to unite it, to bring its strengths together. Your Earth needs uniting, you may have noticed that and certainly an important way of understanding the points which need to be united is by a comprehensive study program focused upon the dimensions. I would suggest that you get a notebook and that you divide it into sections, the 3rd, the 4th, the 5th and the 6th dimensions. If you wish, you may have further sections on the 7th, the 8th, and the 9th dimensions.

First of all then write down particular points that you have understood from the material I have given you on each dimension. Now in your notebook you don't especially want to repeat in the same wording everything I've given in this volume but there may be an experience that you've had which helps you understand a particular dimension. When you recognize a particular dimensional experience in a way that has helped you to clarify your life then write a brief synopsis of it, put it in your notebook. You may, occasionally, be watching television and see a program which relates very clearly to one of the dimensions, write that down in your notebook under the section of that particular dimension.

Gradually you will gather material which will allow you to perhaps teach others, also to understand dimensions. The awakening of a sense of proportion here on the Earth is necessary to have your peaceful Earth. Understanding of proportion only comes when the 6th dimension, and what it represents is seen as the guiding system for the other dimensions. A guidance system is always necessary, it is there when you allow yourself to recognize it.

EXERCISE: On a sheet of paper with a blue pencil or felt pen draw some vertical and horizontal lines so they intersect - at least six in each direction. On another sheet of paper some orange lines which intersect. Now if you can use tissue paper that is transparent - that is thin - it will be helpful. If not, use regular paper. Blue, orange, another that is perhaps green and the fourth brown. Now if you don't like these colors choose four of your own but I am suggesting the blue represent the 6th dimensional energy structure, the orange the 5th, the green the 4th, and the brown the 3rd. When you have completed these four energy structures you may wish to use a light box in connection with them so that you can overlay them and see them together. You could use a window, holding them up, put your brown first, then your green, then your orange and then your blue. Now move them around, not overlaying them exactly so that one hides the other, but slightly askew or slightly varying the placement until you can see all four.

Now I would suggest that you view this rather as a meditative exercise, the brighter the colors you choose the better and the lines need to be firm enough so you can see through your paper.

Now if you cannot find the physical paper and the light box or window, you can visualize this. Visualizing yourself looking through several layers, perhaps for most of you, it will be more helpful to do it on the physical level and after a few times of doing this you may be able to visualize it without using the physical papers. Now remember you want to look then at the blue which represents the 6th dimension and at the energy of the other three dimensions as they come together so seek to see the blue as the uniting factor of the other three. You might see the blue as a point rather like your sun shining into the other three and this lights up the other three energy structures from all points of view. Now you can play with this. Earlier in the book we did some exercises of seeing the 3rd, the 4th, and the 5th dimensions as islands. You could place them side by side like the islands allowing yourself to visualize the blue shining through into all three that are placed side by side. You might do the following as an exercise in creativity.

Let us say you have a goal of unlimited abundance. Seek to focus upon the blue energy grid as that level of unlimited abundance which you would like to manifest in your life. It shines, the blue, which now is electric in your visualization, shines onto the orange, then onto the green and then onto the brown. If you are working with this visualization on the physical level first clarify within your knowingness that the blue has the full unlimited abundance - it holds it. You might even visualize the blue as full of that abundance. You could be creative and see dollar bills focused in that blue or a complete abundant flow of love, a complete abundant flow of energy - perhaps however, simply visualizing the blue as containing every aspect of abundance which has not yet been made physical is the clearest way of using this energy grid system but you can see it as "dripping" with that full abundant level. Then take away that blue sheet of paper but you will know that the blue is shining fully on the other three. In point of fact, the blue has permeated all of the other three - its energy is contacting the other three pieces of paper or perhaps visualized colors.

Now move your paper around, shift it, it would be wise to have the brown, green, and orange in that order - the topmost - the orange and the brown on the bottom with the green in the center but move them around physically, try them so they are almost centered upon one another and spread them a little, keep moving them, you might want to spread them so they just touch. Or perhaps they're half covered up by one another.

What you are looking for my friends is an electrical charge literally almost like a surge of electrical contact that comes back at you through the movement of these energies. What you are looking for my friends is an energy recognition of how best to ignite your own full, unlimited abundance. Now you need to be rather honest with yourself in this exercise. One can imagine immediately that there is this electrical contact, one can have some illusion in regard to what has been accomplished. In my opinion not having any expectation about it but relaxing in as deep a meditative state as possible, even if you're working with the physical pieces of paper and have your eyes open, is the appropriate way to begin with this.

Allow several days doing this exercise for perhaps ten minutes a day - not requiring of it anything - simply allowing the contact, shifting the paper around, being willing to energize the ideal blueprint level of your own full abundance and how to connect it into the 3rd, the 4th, and the 5th dimension in a way that it unifies and flows and is integrated. When you do this then it will need to be done so that, for most of you, slowly, you build a confidence in your ability to contact that fully abundant level, that fully integrated 6th dimensionally focused soul perspective.

When you reach a point that it all comes together for you and there is the electrical surge, this electrical surge will seem to move out from the brown, the green, and the orange, unite beyond color into a surging back to the blue level. It completes the circuit, my friends, and it says to this blue level, "yes, I have united my understanding enough to allow this goal of full abundance to use the structure which has now been fully energized. The structures open - come on in - the flow can use it now." Now keep this in mind - it is certainly possible to open all of it at once but for many of you this type of a flow connection may be gradual. The reason is this: there must be a deep, clear understanding within you of what the 6th dimensional structure and its use by the soul really represents. Many of you talk about unlimitedness and are aware of it but you don't really believe that it can be used by you <u>NOW.</u>

You have accepted at a basic level some limitation and thus you may have to clear from your subconscious mind beliefs about unlimitedness. Many of you are doing this gradually, in a step by step manner. What you will contact then through this exercise is a creative opening which takes you into the next level of abundance which you have allowed yourself to contact. It seems to me well worth using this system if you will, because it helps you to unify your physical, emotional, and mental expressions into an ignitor of the next level of spiritual opportunity that you are open to. It is then a good tool to keep using over and over for any area in which unlimitedness is important for you or even for specific areas which are specific goals which you have in mind.

One way to use it for specific goals is before beginning the exercise as outlined before to simply place your four pieces of paper together or visualize all four lines coming together exactly and then view the type of goal you are seeking right across the energy grid. In other words, use the energy grid - the four leveled energy grid - as a screen. If you wish a loving, fulfilling, relationship view it. View yourself in such a relationship before you begin to utilize the technique I have given. Be as specific as you care to be in this visualization and allow some flexibility within what you are invoking. It will probably help you to manifest such a relationship. If you say to the 6th dimension, "I only want a relationship partner that is, in a man's case, six-feet eight," or in a woman's case, weighs a hundred and five pounds," then you are perhaps limiting or restricting, taking the opportunity down to a point where it is much more difficult to bring it in. Yes, you may get it eventually, but there may be others beside a man six-eight or a woman a hundred and five who would be a good relationship partner for you so at this point you might visualize someone that represents to you the ideal as far as your soul is concerned, someone that will help you fulfill your soul's purposes.

If you are visualizing having a loving relationship in every case, perhaps it is appropriate to ask this level to bring you what is a part of the plan and your purpose within it. Have that as a part of the ideal level.

You can use a clearer and clearer understanding of dimensions to release certain deep resistances that have perhaps been there without your awareness over many, many lifetimes. Let us say that sometimes if you light up an area in a room, in a particular way, the light shining specifically from that room can show you much more clearly who you are than if that room were not as specifically designed for lighting up particular areas. The Divine Plan then has prepared a system for us and we can all learn to use it clearly.

You may have read about telephones that can connect you beyond the Earth and you may have wondered how they work and if they even exist and the point is that they do exist and I am about to tell you how they work.

There is a connection, a flow between the dimensions that is electrical in nature and you are sitting in the 3rd dimension with your telephone and let us say that someone has left the physical level and they are sitting in the 7th dimension with their telephone. You can utilize the 6th dimension as the connecting point and that is because the higher dimensions can reflect into it as a relay station and then project the message into the other dimensions. All angelic beings use this system of reflection.

When you connect with a being such as Michael you are really using several relay points to establish a link into what Michael represents. An angelic being is able to utilize energy structurally a little differently than you can. Although there is perhaps not a framing in of that energy on the 3rd dimension there is certainly a framing in of it on the 4th dimension and thus we could say there is a 9th, 7th, 6th, and 4th dimensional flow which becomes a point of weaving which becomes a means of weaving dimensional possibilities together beyond the "normal" physical way.

Now those of humanity who have very close connections with the angelic kingdom and you may know some of them, seem to have a "light" understanding which transcends what the 3rd dimension seems to put humanity in contact with. The angels speak to you from the 4th dimension but remember again that is a reflection from the 6th, the 7th, and the 9th dimension so they speak to you from the higher perspectives and teach you to connect in beyond mental or physical barriers. Those that are very focused in the 5th dimension and still functioning on the 3rd dimensional Earth have difficulty believing in angels unless they have opened up to allow the 6th dimension to show them that connection and for many of them it is important because it touches into the 4th dimension which is the uniting and flowing perspective they are seeking. I always encourage humanity to play with the angels and it is because their point of view transcends the somewhat structurally stuck points of view that many of humanity yet have.

If you have a favorite angel or archangel you might ask them to play with you visually in a manner which will help you unite the dimensions. A meditation in which you slide around on some of the geometric figures which your clairvoyance may show you on the 5th dimension will help unite the 4th and the 5th because you add movement to the structures in the 5th. The angels can show you how to step into the 4th dimension without fear.

One way to view it, to view life at this time upon the Earth, is that your Earth is really stepping into its angelic connection as it goes into the 4th dimension. Now certainly the angels have been here for humanity through your religions that sought to give you an understanding of the 6th dimension or a religious focus that talked about God the Creator and for many of you in these lives the angels were very real, were your friends and companions.

It is important to play with them again, to be united with them again, and as you visualize your Earth flow into the 4th dimension as we've discussed previously, this is an analogy, not the truth, not the whole picture, because your Earth is seeking to become multi-dimensional but there is a doorway that your Earth is poised in now to a new way of relating to the 4th dimension. You could visualize yourself and truly all of humanity stepping through that doorway and being welcomed by these great angelic beings such as Michael, Auriel, Raphael, Gabriel, Metatron, Sandalphon, Ratziel, Tzaphkiel, Tzadkiel, plus the various groups of angels, the Seraphim, the Cherubim.

The angelic hosts then are so joyous about this opportunity to unite with a wider spectrum of humanity than ever before. They want to see humanity moving through this doorway into a scene where great beings of light welcome humanity not on the spiritual level but on this clearer physical level, this more flowing level which represents what the 4th dimension really is. They want to see humanity taking with them all of the strengths and skills that they've learned, the knowledge, the greater understanding and now using them in this more flowing and therefore more loving environment.

If you will begin to see your Earth entering this new era as a part of the more universal and connected level, you personally can assist in bringing peace to the Earth. You might be very creative with this exercise seeing humanity around the globe celebrating your new Earth, bells ringing everywhere announcing peace, great celebrations, peoples coming together - different cultures uniting, communicating, sharing, caring, assisting each other in a caring manner that doesn't force another culture to accept help but allows what is needed to be there. See then the structure of your Earth responding to the needs of your Earth.

The reason it hasn't always done that is there was no sense of unity, no sense of connection within at least the mass consciousness level which allowed, through that 6th dimensional understanding, peace to unite all perspectives.

Emotional nations, those whose feeling nature really was prevalent didn't always understand a nation whose predominant characteristic was more mental or one whose predominate characteristic was physical.

There wasn't an allowingness through this 6th dimensional perspective which must be overlayed through the qualities of the heart. All qualities of the heart are the uniting characteristics for humanity because they are the overlay system itself. All of them then can be used to allow your Earth to have the type of expression which no longer is at odds with itself through lack of understanding, lack of communication or old fear patterns brought up from the past.

As you travel around the Earth view that particular area you are going through as stepping through a new doorway into a clearer perspective, into a welcoming committee of angelic beings, into a freer more unlimited expression. See your Earth opening to allow communication with other civilizations, other planets, other solar systems, other galaxies, other universes. This too is a part of your future. It is a part of your clearer, more comprehensive understanding of who you are, that indeed you are not a small isolated planet or "the center of the universe." That has been your personality level talking to you, the ego of your planet saying "we are all that exists." It is time to move to the soul level of planetary understanding so that you may unite creatively with all members of the galactic and universal federations which are there to express as divine beings just as you are.

It is wonderful to allow the movement to enter the 4th dimension and to flow it through the 5th dimension reflected of course from the 6th. Allow the foundation of what you've learned 3rd dimensionally to be there also so that you may open up your universality on the physical level. This will bring you those scientific breakthrough's you are looking for, those wonderful ways of expressing that you have not yet allowed.

Because, my friends, you are members of a greater perspective and the other members are waiting in the wings to share with you their points of view, their understanding and to learn and grow from you also. They've been a little afraid of this rather war-like planet. Some have come and not survived the trip, others have been rejected and forced to leave. It's time to open up the door and allow in the members of your cosmic family. They are not strangers. They are friends and neighbors united with you in creating a wonderful, peaceful co-creator existence, certainly on your Earth, but perhaps more importantly, on the universal level.

I am truly excited about our energy adventure and I invite you to write to the Foundation and share the results of the uses of some of the exercises. The Foundation has a newsletter which can be subscribed to and I promise you this - that if you will write and share what you are getting from this dimensional book - some of your experiences will be published in the newsletter so that others may also gain a clearer understanding from your activities. It can be published with your name or without it so if you do write in please say if the Foundation may use your name.

It is then a privilege to have had this opportunity to discuss dimensions with you. You might wish to also write to me, Vywamus, care of the Foundation and tell me what sort of material you personally would like to see written about in a book. Certainly we seek to be open to the needs of humanity. I give you in the volumes I am writing through Janet what I see as important but I invite you to share those areas which seem to you to need further clarification and understanding in such a volume as this.

Recognize my friends, that we of the spiritual hierarchy are available for you to channel and part of the Foundation's responsibilities lies in teaching the channeling process. Please inquire if you are interested.

My love to you,

Vywamus

Forever Numerology

Includes Master Numbers 11–99!
by Lynn Buess

In *Forever Numerology*, Lynn Buess again takes a gigantic leap for numerology with extraordinary new insights and methods of interpretation. This volume will define new standards for years to come. You will be swept through transcendent realms of light and awareness, even as Buess's solid psychological base and down-to-earth reality keep you centered right here in the present moment.

Having practiced for decades as a psychotherapist, Buess has uncovered deeply repressed blocks and negative unconscious complexes in many of his clients. In this book, he works some of his insights for recognizing dysfunction into the interpretation of numerology in the hopes of awakening new seekers to the dark side of the self. Once you recognize this dark side, you have the possibility of working it out of your life. The interpretations and experiences presented in this book are given through the symbolic wisdom of numbers.

Truly, no complete volume can be written on any subject; however, this book comes closer than ever to portraying the evolution of consciousness through the symbology of numbers. It will be of help in your journey through life and in your search for the meaning of numbers.

17^{95} SOFTCOVER 290 P. ISBN 1-891824-65-1

Numerology for the New Age
By Lynn Buess

Our own vibrations or cyclical patterns are numerologically determined by our date of birth and given name. By understanding these cycles, we can learn to more effectively express our potential, human and divine. This volume concentrates more upon the experiential value of numerology than the historical.

$11.00 SOFTCOVER 262 P. ISBN 0-929385-31-4

Numerology: Nuances in Relationships
By Lynn Buess

Welcome to a new and meaningful application of numbers in your life. This volume is written to assist you in your quest to better understand yourself in relation to another person. You will discover many new insights and avenues toward more mature and compatible interactions with others.

$13.75 SOFTCOVER 309 P. ISBN 0-929385-23-3

Children of Light, Children of Denial
By Lynn Buess

There is a rapid and expansive awakening within the self-awareness movement that integration of self includes a harmonious dance between the light (conscious) and dark (unconscious) aspects of human nature. Lynn Buess addresses the cycle of denial that leads to so much dysfunction in our time.

$8.95 SOFTCOVER 125 P. ISBN 0-929385-15-2

Phone: 928-526-1345 or 1-800-450-0985 • Fax 928-714-1132

. . . or use our online bookstore at www.lighttechnology.com

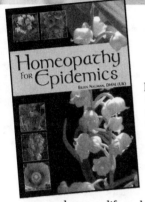

THE EXPLORER RACE SERIES

ZOOSH AND HIS FRIENDS THROUGH ROBERT SHAPIRO

THE SERIES: Humans—creators-in-training—have a purpose and destiny so heartwarmingly, profoundly glorious that it is almost unbelievable from our present dimensional perspective. Humans are great lightbeings from beyond this creation, gaining experience in dense physicality. This truth about the great human genetic experiment of the Explorer Race and the mechanics of creation is being revealed for the first time by Zoosh and his friends through superchannel Robert Shapiro. These books read like adventure stories as we follow the clues from this creation that we live in out to the Council of Creators and beyond.

❶ THE EXPLORER RACE

You individuals reading this are truly a result of the genetic experiment on Earth. You are beings who uphold the principles of the Explorer Race. The information in this book is designed to show you who you are and give you an evolutionary understanding of your past that will help you now. The key to empowerment in these days is to not know everything about your past, but to know what will help you now. Your number-one function right now is your status of Creator apprentice, which you have achieved through years and lifetimes of sweat. You are constantly being given responsibilities by the Creator that would normally be things that Creator would do. The responsibility and the destiny of the Explorer Race is not only to explore, but to create. 574 P. $25.00 ISBN 0-929385-38-1

❷ ETs and the EXPLORER RACE

In this book, Robert channels Joopah, a Zeta Reticulan now in the ninth dimension who continues the story of the great experiment—the Explorer Race—from the perspective of his civilization. The Zetas would have been humanity's future selves had not humanity re-created the past and changed the future. 237 P. $14.95 ISBN 0-929385-79-9

❸ EXPLORER RACE: ORIGINS and the NEXT 50 YEARS

This volume has so much information about who we are and where we came from—the source of male and female beings, the war of the sexes, the beginning of the linear mind, feelings, the origin of souls—it is a treasure trove. In addition, there is a section that relates to our near future—how the rise of global corporations and politics affects our future, how to use benevolent magic as a force of creation and how we will go out to the stars and affect other civilizations. Astounding information. 339 P. $14.95 ISBN 0-929385-95-0

❹ EXPLORER RACE: CREATORS and FRIENDS
The MECHANICS of CREATION

Now that you have a greater understanding of who you are in the larger sense, it is necessary to remind you of where you came from, the true magnificence of your being. You must understand that you are creators-in-training, and yet you were once a portion of Creator. One could certainly say, without being magnanimous, that you are still a portion of Creator, yet you are training for the individual responsibility of being a creator, to give your Creator a coffee break. This book will allow you to understand the vaster qualities and help you remember the nature of the desires that drive any creator, the responsibilities to which a creator must answer, the reaction a creator must have to consequences and the ultimate reward of any creator. 435 P. $19.95 ISBN 1-891824-01-5

❺ EXPLORER RACE: PARTICLE PERSONALITIES

All around you in every moment you are surrounded by the most magical and mystical beings. They are too small for you to see as single individuals, but in groups you know them as the physical matter of your daily life. Particles who might be considered either atoms or portions of atoms consciously view the vast spectrum of reality yet also have a sense of personal memory like your own linear memory. These particles remember where they have been and what they have done in their infinitely long lives. Some of the particles we hear from are Gold, Mountain Lion, Liquid Light, Uranium, the Great Pyramid's Capstone, This Orb's Boundary, Ice and Ninth-Dimensional Fire. 237 P. $14.95 ISBN 0-929385-97-7

❻ EXPLORER RACE and BEYOND

With a better idea of how creation works, we go back to the Creator's advisers and receive deeper and more profound explanations of the roots of the Explorer Race. The liquid Domain and the Double Diamond portal share lessons given to the roots on their way to meet the Creator of this universe, and finally the roots speak of their origins and their incomprehensibly long journey here. 360 P. $14.95 ISBN 1-891824-06-6

THE EXPLORER RACE SERIES

ZOOSH AND HIS FRIENDS THROUGH ROBERT SHAPIRO

❼ EXPLORER RACE: The COUNCIL of CREATORS

The thirteen core members of the Council of Creators discuss their adventures in coming to awareness of themselves and their journeys on the way to the Council on this level. They discuss the advice and oversight they offer to all creators, including the Creator of this local universe. These beings are wise, witty and joyous, and their stories of Love's Creation create an expansion of our concepts as we realize that we live in an expanded, multiple-level reality. 237 P. $14.95 ISBN 1-891824-13-9

❽ EXPLORER RACE and ISIS

This is an amazing book! It has priestess training, Shamanic training, Isis's adventures with Explorer Race beings—before Earth and on Earth—and an incredibly expanded explanation of the dynamics of the Explorer Race. Isis is the prototypal loving, nurturing, guiding feminine being, the focus of feminine energy. She has the ability to expand limited thinking without making people with limited beliefs feel uncomfortable. She is a fantastic storyteller, and all of her stories are teaching stories. If you care about who you are, why you are here, where you are going and what life is all about—pick up this book. You won't lay it down until you are through, and then you will want more. 317 P. $14.95 ISBN 1-891824-11-2

❾ EXPLORER RACE and JESUS

The core personality of that being known on the Earth as Jesus, along with his students and friends, describes with clarity and love his life and teaching two thousand years ago. He states that his teaching is for all people of all races in all countries. Jesus announces here for the first time that he and two others, Buddha and Mohammed, will return to Earth from their place of being in the near future, and a fourth being, a child already born now on Earth, will become a teacher and prepare humanity for their return. So heartwarming and interesting, you won't want to put it down. 354 P. $16.95 ISBN 1-891824-14-7

❿ EXPLORER RACE: Earth History and Lost Civilization

Speaks of Many Truths and Zoosh, through Robert Shapiro, explain that planet Earth, the only water planet in this solar system, is on loan from Sirius as a home and school for humanity, the Explorer Race. Earth's recorded history goes back only a few thousand years, its archaeological history a few thousand more. Now this book opens up as if a light was on in the darkness, and we see the incredible panorama of brave souls coming from other planets to settle on different parts of Earth. We watch the origins of tribal groups and the rise and fall of civilizations, and we can begin to understand the source of the wondrous diversity of plants, animals and humans that we enjoy here on beautiful Mother Earth. 310 P. $14.95 ISBN 1-891824-20-1

⓫ EXPLORER RACE: ET VISITORS SPEAK

Even as you are searching the sky for extraterrestrials and their spaceships, ETs are here on planet Earth—they are stranded, visiting, exploring, studying the culture, healing the Earth of trauma brought on by irresponsible mining or researching the history of Christianity over the past two thousand years. Some are in human guise, and some are in spirit form. Some look like what we call animals as they come from the species' home planet and interact with their fellow beings—those beings that we have labeled cats or cows or elephants. Some are brilliant cosmic mathematicians with a sense of humor; they are presently living here as penguins. Some are fledgling diplomats training for future postings on Earth when we have ET embassies here. In this book, these fascinating beings share their thoughts, origins and purposes for being here. 350 P. $14.95 ISBN 1-891824-28-7

⓬ EXPLORER RACE: Techniques for GENERATING SAFETY

Wouldn't you like to generate safety so you could go wherever you need to go and do whatever you need to do in a benevolent, safe and loving way for yourself? Learn safety as a radiated environment that will allow you to gently take the step into the new timeline, into a benevolent future and away from a negative past. 208 P. $9.95 ISBN 1-891824-26-0

Phone: 928-526-1345 or 1-800-450-0985 • Fax 928-714-1132

... or use our online bookstore at www.lighttechnology.com

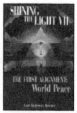

Publishing Presents

Plus Hundreds More!

A New Formula For Creation
Judith Moore

This book brings an inspiring positive message regarding the future of our planet. Earth is experiencing the Shift of the Ages, a time marked by massive Earth changes and social upheaval. This is foretold in many prophecies, including Hopi prophecies and the biblical Revelations. They warn that raising consciousness is the only way to avert a massive cataclysm.

$16.95 Softcover, 186 p. ISBN: 1-891824-57-0

Living in the Heart
(With CD)
Drunvalo Melchizedek

This is a book of remembering. You have always had this place within your heart, and it is still there now. It existed before creation, and it will exist even after the last star shines its brilliant light. This book is written with the least amount of words possible to convey the meaning and to keep the integrity of the essence of this experience. The images are purposefully simple. It is written from the heart, not the mind.

$25.00 Softcover, 120 p. ISBN: 1-891824-43-0

Ancient Secret of the Flower of Life *Vol. I*
Drunvalo Melchizedek

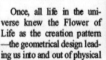

Once, all life in the universe knew the Flower of Life as the creation pattern —the geometrical design leading us into and out of physical existence. Sacred Geometry is the form beneath our being and points to a divine order in our reality. We can follow that order from the invisible atom to the infinite stars, finding ourselves at each step.

$25.00 Softcover, 228 p. ISBN: 1-891824-17-1

Change Your Encodements, Your DNA, Your Life!
Amma through
Cathy Chapman

The first part of this book discusses what you call love. Love is the most powerful energy. The second part contains powerful techniques for working with your DNA encodements. The third part contains what some call predictions, which are nothing more than my reading and interpretation of the energy at the time when the energy was read.

$16.95 Softcover, 303 p. ISBN: 1-891824-52-X

Animal Souls Speak
Explorer Race Series
Robert Shapiro

Welcome to the footsteps of the loving beings (animals) who support you, who wish to reveal more about themselves to you and who welcome you, not only to planet Earth, but more specifically to the pathway of self-discovery. The animal world will speak through elders, since that way they can include knowledge and wisdom about their home planets. Each animal brings a wonderous gift to share with humanity—enjoy it!

$29.95 Softcover, 610 p. ISBN: 1-891824-50-3

Ancient Secret of the Flower of Life *Vol. II*
Drunvalo Melchizedek

Drunvalo shares the instructions for the Mer-Ka-Ba meditation, step-by-step techniques for the re-creation of the energy field of the evolved human. From the pyramids and mysteries of Egypt to the new race of Indigo children, Drunvalo presents the sacred geometries of the Reality and the subtle energies that shape our world.

$25.00 Softcover, 477 p. ISBN: 1-891824-21-X

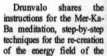

. . . or use our online bookstore at www.lighttechnology.com

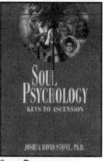

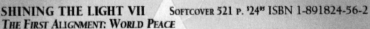

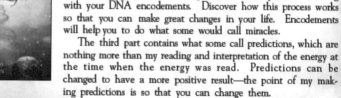

CROP CIRCLES REVEALED
LANGUAGE OF THE LIGHT SYMBOLS

BARBARA LAMB, MS, MFL
JUDITH K. MOORE

$25⁰⁰

SOFTCOVER 308 P.
ISBN 1-891824-32-5

Welcome to the world of crop circles, one of the most TANTALIZING phenomena in our world today. It is difficult not to be captivated by their beauty and complexity and by the questions and issues they provoke, including one that becomes more pressing everyday—what other INTELLIGENT life forms are out there trying to communicate with us? What are their intentions? What is the communication system between them, the Earth and humanity? Unlock the secret keys for the emergence of a new world of peace, freedom, healing and unconditional love. We are being assisted with energy never before to REGENERATE ourselves and our ailing planet. Reactivate and discover our invaluable gifts and divine mission. Awaken your DNA and empower yourself! This comprehensive document reveals the deep mysteries of the crop circle phenomenon. Scientific analysis of the hoaxing controversy and high-level spiritual transmissions are combined in the masterful presentation for your use and interpretation.

MAHATMA I & II
The I AM Presence

BRIAN GRATTAN

Awaken and realize that all of humankind will create their "body for ascension," whether they accomplish this now or later, and that this is not the exclusive domain of Christ or Buddha or the many others who have ascended—*this is your birthright*. When humans lift the veils of their unworthiness and recognize that they are the sons of God, that there is divine equality and that no one is greater than another, then you will have begun your journey in the way that it was intended. The *Mahatma* is for those who are motivated to search for the answers that can respond to their mental and spiritual bodies. No matter how contrary our current beliefs, this book contains methods for creating your spiritual lightbody for ascension and also explains your eternal journey in a way never before available to humankind.

SOFTCOVER 480 P. $19⁹⁵ ISBN 0-929385-77-2

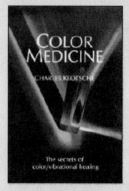

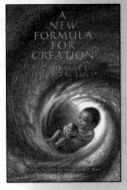

The Amethyst Light

Djwhal Khul through Violet Starre

Perhaps you are thumbing through the pages of this little book, wondering if it contains the insights you are looking for. Who is Ascended Master Djwhal Khul? Will this book be useful to you? Will it help you to understand metaphysics and present time in Earth history? Will it help you in life?

I was a Tibetan Buddhist monk. I ran a monastery. In that life I focused on meditation, study, simple chores and teaching. The contemplative life helps to raise consciousness and provides a testing ground for how well principles have been learned. In my Tibetan incarnation I sought my true Buddha nature to demonstrate compassion for all sentient beings and to break free of reincarnation and join the Noble Ones. I write not as a man incarnated on Earth, but as a member of the spiritual hierarchy, for the benefit of all. Join me in this work.

$14⁹⁵   Softcover 128 P.
ISBN 1-891824-41-4

The Diamond Light

Djwhal Khul through Violet Starre

This book presents esoteric teachings similar to those given to Alice A. Bailey between the two great world wars and offers them in short, concise and simple form. The original teachings from Master Djwhal Khul were presented in lengthy volumes that were difficult to understand without a deep background in Theosophy, founded by Madame Blavatsky in the late nineteenth century. The Master wishes now to offer a short, clear and accessible text for the general New Age reader.

The Master is one member of a planetary council of spiritual beings who exist within another dimension and guide the spiritual destiny of this planet and its life forms. Although this spiritual government exists, it does not interfere with the free will of humanity but occasionally sends such teachers to guide us.

The Master is accessible to all and does not reserve his communication only for the most advanced souls. He is available to those who most desperately need him, who feel as if they are struggling to survive in the modern world without a message of hope. That message can be found here.

$14⁹⁵   Softcover 154 P.
ISBN 1-891824-25-2

Phone: 928-526-1345 or 1-800-450-0985 • Fax 928-714-1132
... or use our online bookstore at www.lighttechnology.com

Shamanic Secrets Mastery Series

Speaks of Many Truths and Reveals the Mysteries through Robert Shapiro

This book explores the heart and soul connection between humans and Mother Earth. Through that intimacy, miracles of healing and expanded awareness can flourish. To heal the planet and be healed as well, we can lovingly extend our energy selves out to the mountains and rivers and intimately bond with the Earth. Gestures and vision can activate our hearts to return us to a healthy, caring relationship with the land we live on. The character of some of Earth's most powerful features is explored and understood, with exercises given to connect us with those places. As we project our love and healing energy there, we help the Earth to heal from human destruction of the planet and its atmosphere. Dozens of photographs, maps and drawings assist the process in twenty-five chapters, which cover the Earth's more critical locations.

498 p. $19.95 ISBN 1-891824-12-0

Learn to understand the sacred nature of your own physical body and some of the magnificent gifts it offers you. When you work with your physical body in these new ways, you will discover not only its sacredness, but how it is compatible with Mother Earth, the animals, the plants, even the nearby planets, all of which you now recognize as being sacred in nature. It is important to feel the value of oneself physically before one can have any lasting physical impact on the world. If a physical energy does not feel good about itself, it will usually be resolved; other physical or spiritual energies will dissolve it because it is unnatural. The better you feel about your physical self when you do the work in the previous book as well as this one and the one to follow, the greater and more lasting will be the benevolent effect on your life, on the lives of those around you and ultimately on your planet and universe.

576 p. $25.00 ISBN 1-891824-29-5

Spiritual mastery encompasses many different means to assimilate and be assimilated by the wisdom, feelings, flow, warmth, function and application of all beings in your world that you will actually contact in some way. A lot of spiritual mastery has been covered in different bits and pieces throughout all the books we've done. My approach to spiritual mastery, though, will be as grounded as possible in things that people on Earth can use—but it won't include the broad spectrum of spiritual mastery, like levitation and invisibility. I'm trying to teach you things that you can actually use and benefit from. My life is basically going to represent your needs, and it gets out the secrets that have been held back in a storylike fashion, so that it is more interesting."

—Speaks of Many Truths through Robert Shapiro

768 p. $29.95 ISBN 1-891824-58-9

THE ANCIENT SECRET OF THE FLOWER OF LIFE
VOLUME 1

THE ANCIENT SECRET
OF THE FLOWER OF LIFE
VOLUME 2

The sacred Flower of Life pattern, the primary geometric generator of all physical form, is explored in even more depth in this volume, the second half of the famed Flower of Life workshop. The proportions of the human body, the nuances of human consciousness, the sizes and distances of the stars, planets and moons, even the creations of humankind, are all shown to reflect their origins in this beautiful and divine image. Through an intricate and detailed geometrical mapping, Drunvalo Melchizedek shows how the seemingly simple design of the Flower of Life contains the genesis of our entire third-dimensional existence.

From the pyramids and mysteries of Egypt to the new race of Indigo children, Drunvalo presents the sacred geometries of the Reality and the subtle energies that shape our world. We are led through a divinely inspired labyrinth of science and stories, logic and coincidence, on a path of remembering where we come from and the wonder and magic of who we are.

Finally, for the first time in print, Drunvalo shares the instructions for the Mer-Ka-Ba meditation, step-by-step techniques for the re-creation of the energy field of the evolved human, which is the key to ascension and the next dimensional world. If done from love, this ancient process of breathing prana opens up for us a world of tantalizing possibility in this dimension, from protective powers to the healing of oneself, of others and even of the planet.

$2500
Softcover 252 P.
ISBN 1-891824-21-X

- The Unfolding of the Third Informational System
- Whispers from Our Ancient Heritage
- Unveiling the Mer-ka-ba Meditation
- Using Your Mer-ka-ba
- Connecting to the Levels of Self
- Two Cosmic Experiments
- What We May Expect in the Forthcoming Dimensional Shift

Available from your favorite bookstore or:

LIGHT TECHNOLOGY PUBLISHING
PO Box 3540 • Flagstaff, AZ 86003